Grace 'y

You a'

amazing young

d your Leadership

Journey will be

EPIC!

Love
Dad

THE LEADERSHIP MANIFESTO

The
Leadership
Manifesto

Eight Steps for
Professional Development

Bill Hicks

LIONCREST
PUBLISHING

THE LEADERSHIP MANIFESTO

Eight Steps for Professional Development

ISBN   978-1-61961-794-0 *Hardcover*

978-1-61961-795-7 *Ebook*

To Joanie for being the wife I could only wish for
and to our amazing children, Grace, Rob,
Kelsey, Ashley, Danny, and Michael.

Contents

Introduction

When I was starting out in my career, I didn't have a coach or a mentor to guide me along the way. I had to learn the hard way, by making mistakes.

I remember at my first job, fresh out of college, I received a phone call one day and was told I was needed to lead a new project. The anxiety of the first test in my career was right in front of me, and honestly, I had no one to turn to. I was new to all of this and did not have leadership allies to guide me. Who would I turn to for advice, but more importantly confidence? The only person was my boss, and honestly, he was only interested in the business, not me or my growth. Have you ever been there before?

I was fortunate that the project went well, the firm earned

money, and we were awarded a second contract. Not long after that, another client came along with a similar but bigger project, and I was put in charge of a team of twelve people. Eventually, I was hired by that client to join their company.

During that time, as I was developing my skills as a manager, I had no one to turn to for moral support and advice. I learned through trial and error. It was challenging to manage people more senior than me. Having to tell someone who was twenty-five years older that he wasn't living up to the job was intimidating.

At first I didn't do anything when staff members were unproductive. I was afraid and intimidated, but finally, the situation became unacceptable. I realized that I was going to fail if they didn't deliver, so I started having the tough conversations I'd been avoiding. Over time, I gained the team's respect because they realized that it took courage to challenge them.

While learning from one's mistakes can be effective, I believe that people become better leaders when they receive guidance and encouragement. I wish I would have had someone to boost my confidence when I was younger. I'm sure I would have become a better leader sooner, if there had been a coach or a mentor in my life.

That's why I decided to write this book. My hope is that it will serve as a virtual mentor to aspiring leaders who have no one to counsel and support them. I hope this book will inspire skillful leaders everywhere to begin mentoring people in their companies who can benefit from their knowledge and assistance.

THE REWARDS OF MENTORSHIP

There is nothing more rewarding than seeing colleagues excel. I find it exciting to help others grow professionally. As a mentor, I'm not responsible in the same way I am as a team manager, and I enjoy being a friend to someone who is ambitious and eager to learn.

I don't remember exactly when I became a mentor. It happened naturally. When I moved to the company where I am now, Ultimate Software, I discovered a very different attitude toward helping others. At my previous job, everyone was focused on their own work and mentoring wasn't encouraged. At Ultimate Software, mentoring is part of the company's DNA.

After I'd been at Ultimate Software awhile, people outside of my department started asking me for feedback, for my opinion, or for help. At first I wondered why they were coming to me instead of their manager, but then I realized that they were looking for a mentor. Though coaching is not an expectation or a part of our professional duties, it is our company culture to be supportive when we can, to help others succeed, and to encourage the development of leadership skills.

THE LEADERSHIP MANIFESTO

In my years as a manager and coach to colleagues young and old, I have observed that there are eight essential disciplines that every successful leader has to master. I refer to these eight disciplines as the Leadership Manifesto. They identify the key skills and qualities of leadership.

Each chapter in this book addresses one of the eight disciplines. Through a dialogue between a mentor named Bill and a mentee named Jennifer, the reason why each discipline is pertinent to leadership is explained, and ways of putting the relevant skill into practice are discussed. The book can be read as a single, evolving narrative or consulted on a chapter-by-chapter basis to focus on a particular aspect of leadership development.

To be a leader means to grow continually. This book is intended to assist new and accomplished leaders in the pursuit of ongoing development. When team members see a manager striving to become a better person and growing professionally, they will be inspired to do the same. If a leader stagnates, so will the team.

THE EIGHT DISCIPLINES

1. **Be yourself.** Build your personal brand and culture.
2. **Speak up.** Express confidence. It's impossible to be a successful leader without it.
3. **Get involved.** Grow socially outside the workplace and develop a network of advocates.
4. **Give and serve.** Give your best to everyone, including management, peers, partners, and customers.
5. **Accept responsibility.** Help those who report to you do better and value their relationship with you.
6. **Lead the way.** Develop your team and cultivate team spirit.
7. **Build structure.** Organize your team so that everyone thrives.
8. **Create relationships.** Lead in the outside world through partnerships with others.

MEET JENNIFER

In the dialogues between Bill and Jennifer that unfold in these pages, you'll find true-to-life scenarios between a mentor and mentee. Each chapter conveys the quality of conversations that build constructive and productive mentoring relationships.

Jennifer encapsulates a number of people whom I have mentored over the years. Her issues and concerns are the same as those most people face when they rise to leadership positions in their companies. Her challenges are typical of employees in all types of business contexts.

Like so many people I've worked with, Jennifer believes she has potential. She has a good reputation in her organization but was recently passed over when a leadership position became available, which is why she reached out to Bill for mentoring.

In each chapter, Jennifer brings to her sessions with Bill a situation that she needs help with. The advice Bill gives her uncovers the value and relevancy of one of the eight leadership disciplines and includes practical exercises for incorporating new skills into her day-to-day work life. As the mentorship progresses, Bill gives Jennifer feedback and directs her attention to the progress she is making and the nuances of what she is learning. His goal is to help Jennifer grow as a leader. At the end of each chapter, Bill recaps the key features of the leadership discipline he presented.

By the end of this book, Jennifer becomes a confident leader who is progressing in her career—as you will be, too, when you put the Leadership Manifesto into practice!

Chapter 1

---- ✹ ----

Be Yourself: Building Your Personal Brand and Culture

"Let me tell you about my first experience as a leader, Jennifer. When I was in my midtwenties I was asked to manage a small team of analysts for a special project. Both of my team members were in their midfifties, with one of them focused on her next break and the other focused on giving me advice like he was my father. I hated the role! How did I get put in charge? I thought this would be fun and exciting. And the worse part, both of these folks were better analysts than me, and I am sure they knew it.

"This was my first supervisor role and I knew that I did not like doing it and was probably not very good at it. This was not what I ever imagined being a leader would be like. I went to my boss for advice, and his only interest was for me to get the work done, so he was no help. I went to the client thinking he could help, and honestly, I think he was hoping I would fail so he could take back the project.

"With this as my introduction to leadership, it's hard to believe I am still in leadership after such a frustrating start. But I did survive my introduction into management, and I have been doing it for close to thirty years. So with that, tell me about yourself and why you wanted to meet."

Jennifer could feel her heart racing. "Bill, you are already starting to make me have doubts about wanting to be a leader. But I wanted to meet with you because I know I want to be a leader.

"I started here at Flagler Health Care right out of college, and I have been here for almost three years. I am a project manager in the Shared Services division, and I truly feel I am professionally on the right track. Lately I have been given the opportunity to manage some critical, large projects, and I was told my performance has been strong."

"That's great," said Bill.

"Thank you. Everyone tells me I am doing a great job here

at Flagler. My reviews are good, my internal customers tell me they like my work. I have developed a nice group of work friends here, and by all accounts I am in a great situation. I am very happy here, but I know I want more. Last month I applied for a manager's position, and I did not even make it past the first round of interviews. I have lost some of my confidence. I was venting to someone I trust here at Flagler, and he suggested I find a mentor and recommended you."

Bill jumps in, "Thank you for the vote of confidence and the interest. As you may know, my role here is on the executive team in finance. Since Flagler does encourage cross-departmental mentoring, I do a fair amount of mentoring. Before we met, I asked around about you."

"You did?" Jennifer asked.

"And I heard good things," Bill continued. "So I am intrigued to explore being a mentor for you. Let's get together again in a few weeks and spend some focus time to see if a partnership makes sense."

FIRST SESSION: WHAT IS YOUR BRAND?

After a few weeks, Jennifer enters Bill's office for their first official mentoring session. "What do you hope to get out of a mentoring experience? What are your goals?"

Jennifer replied that the next time a management position became available in her area, she wanted a viable chance of getting the job. Even more importantly, she wanted to know that she had done everything she could to be the right candidate for the position. She felt that working with a mentor would help her develop professionally.

The response is encouraging and confident. She has a good track record and is focused on her future. Bill is convinced he'll mentor Jennifer and continues the dialogue: "So what personal brand and personal culture do you want to project?"

Jennifer is somewhat taken aback and confused. "What do you mean by personal culture and brand? I kind of understand the brand part, but I don't know what personal culture is."

"Think about a product or service that you admire. Is it the advertising you like? Do you like interacting with the people associated with a particular product or service? Perhaps there's someone who truly impresses you."

Bill pauses and gives Jennifer time to reflect. Then she mentions Subaru.

"What is it about Subaru that makes you admire them?"

"They do the right thing," she says. "They're not just about their product but about how they take care of the world. They appear to be charitable and are concerned about the betterment of everyone, not just themselves." Looking at the broader world we all share is important to Jennifer.

"Okay, so you like the brand. And what do you think their culture is like?"

"I envision it being a culture of doing the right thing, making things better, and striving for the best. I think they have a culture of excellence and positivity."

"Jennifer, you just described an organization that means a lot to you. You mentioned how you see the brand and how you think the company culture must be. Brand deals with how a product or a person is seen by the outside world. Culture, on the other hand, whether it's a company's or an individual's, deals with the internal world. We all, as human beings, have an inside world. Our inner world is expressed in how we think, how we operate, and how we react to challenging or stressful situations.

"Now let's consider your brand. How do people see you? How do your friends see you? What kind of culture do you project to your coworkers? What would they say if someone asked them what they think of you?"

Brand is what's seen from the outside, while culture is the internal foundation, whether for a business or a person.

Bill continues, "For example, I want people at work to view me as being a good leader and a coach. That would be the goal of my brand. After they get to know me, I'd hope they might say that I inspire a culture of collaboration, one that's about working together, creating a team, and doing the right thing. So in your role as a project manager, Jennifer, do you feel that you're outgoing?"

"Absolutely," she says. "I work with people all day long and thrive on the energy that comes from it. I also like making improvements, both at home on projects or at work, making our company better."

"Okay, and if you had to work on a production line building computer systems, would that make you happy?"

"No, I like interacting with people and would suffer without it."

"Good," Bill responds, "you're in a job that suits your personality. Your brand is going to work well for you. You're fortunate to be in that situation. There are a lot of people who feel they're in a position that doesn't match who they are. For those individuals, I encourage them to find a role that aligns with their internal culture and to elevate their brand.

"Now let's talk about the people who work with you. What do you think they think of you? How do they view you?"

"Well," Jennifer replies, "a lot of times I think they feel that I'm early in my career and that I'm not growing much. Often at Flagler, I work with people who are senior to me, and sometimes I get insecure in those situations.

"I feel I'm not as confident as I should be, and I hurt my career because of it. I don't have the same reputation that I have with my friends. I think I'm viewed at work as being more introverted than I'd like to be."

Bill challenges Jennifer at this point, "In our first meeting, you stated you were ready to move into management and were upset that you didn't get the opportunity. Now you're saying the team views you in a way that may mean you're not ready. Can you see why personal brand and culture are so important? You view yourself one way, and the outside world views you another. Our goal is to create alignment between the two."

Jennifer's body language starts to relax as she begins to understand what Bill is pointing to. In an effort to direct the attention away from herself, she asks Bill, "What was it like for you, Bill, when you had been out of school for five years? Were you in a similar situation? What was your brand?"

Bill responds, "I actually was a computer science major at school and did well. My first few years out, I was a computer programmer. Strange, isn't it, now that I'm in finance and accounting? That's because I was a complete failure as a computer programmer!"

After letting his confession sink in, Bill continues, "I went to school for one thing, did well, and then came out and failed. I realized being a computer programmer was harder than I expected. While I had an analytical mind, I was not an engineer, and the role didn't fit. I struggled for over a year with what to do about it until a metric analyst role opened up in the finance department, and I jumped at it.

"When I moved into my new role, I realized I needed to switch my mindset to one of success, which was hard for me to do, feeling the weight of failure in my previous role. My confidence was not where it needed to be. I had to change how I felt internally and how people saw me. I wanted to be successful and never again have to feel a sense of failure in my career."

Bill continues by saying that he also wanted his brand to be someone who was always willing to help. "I may not have always had the right answer, but I always felt that I was viewed as someone who worked hard and was willing to lend a hand. That's how I wanted people to see me. I was also conscious about not stepping into other people's roles.

"Whenever an opportunity presented itself, regardless of how challenging it may have been, I took advantage of it. I became known as a go-to person, though I didn't seek that out or do it on purpose. I was just willing to help out, whether it was doing some proofreading, reviewing a report, or sitting in for a colleague who was on vacation. I was the guy who was willing to take notes in a meeting. Whatever it was, I made myself available. Over time, I built a brand and developed a reputation of genuinely caring about other people's success. At the same time, I never felt afraid to ask my peers for help if I needed it."

He goes on, "Jennifer, let me give you another example, one from someone I just finished mentoring. I've been speaking about things that happened to me twenty-five or thirty years ago. I want to share with you an experience from the last few years.

"Jonathan works out of our California office, so I was mentoring him mostly on the phone rather than in person. He was someone whom everyone saw as a rising star.

"Jonathan's goal in life was to become an executive. It had been his lifelong dream to get an MBA from a prestigious university. When he came to me, he was he ready to quit his job, take a two-year pause, and move to the other side of the country to go to an Ivy League school.

"Hearing about his ambitions, I encouraged Jonathan to take six months and throw himself fully into his job—to give it everything he had to see where it took him. I told him to always help out and do the right thing. If there was a trip that no one wanted to take, he should offer to go. He should be the person that people could rely on.

"After six months, if an opening didn't come along, then I would encourage him to seek his dream and go for a master's degree. I felt that by devoting time and effort to being the go-to person for his organization, he might be able to find an executive opportunity. I also wanted Jonathan to be confident and not worry that he was starting out in his career. I felt it was important that he not be labeled as a millennial or a rookie, but should be seen instead as someone who wanted to help the organization be the best it could be. But I made no promises.

"Fast forward six months. Jonathan put in the effort, traveled a lot, and never took credit for any of it. By chance, a director position came along, and everyone in the company felt that Jonathan was the right person for the job. After going through the interviewing process, it was obvious Jonathan was the right choice, and he was promoted to director. He had earned it. He had done everything for all the right reasons—not for personal benefit, but for the success of the organization. He made himself available and did not have to get a MBA in order to succeed."

> The purpose of not labeling someone as a millennial is so their brand is one of a trusted employee, regardless of their age.

By now, Jennifer is caught up in the conversation. Things had worked out better for Jonathan than he could have wished. In far less time than it would have taken him to earn an additional degree, he had become an executive in a growing company.

"That's an amazing story!" Jennifer enthuses.

"Now are you beginning to understand why your brand and your culture are so important?" Bill asks. "Everything and everyone has a brand or a reputation based on how people view them. Think about your friends outside of work. How do they view you?

"Do you like what you are projecting to the world? Do you like Jennifer's brand with her friends? If the answer is yes, then congratulations. If the answer is no, you should have a road map for how you are going to change things. The key point is I don't want you to project a brand or a culture that's not you. Your brand has to reflect who you really are because: (1) if not, it's not sustainable, and (2) you don't want to be viewed as not being genuine. If there's one thing you need to understand about projecting a brand or culture, it's that it must be true to who you are. You may want to tweak or modify a few things here and there, and that's okay. What you don't want to do is overhaul your brand. Does that make sense?"

"Yes, I get it. My brand is something that I shouldn't fake; it has to be aligned to how I am," Jennifer replies.

"Right. Now I'm going to give you your first homework assignment. I want you to take some time and consider the qualities and traits that make up the brand and culture you want to represent. You can do this by thinking about and identifying the characteristics of all your interactions with people, the books you read, films you see, and so forth—basically, everything you do. Then decide which of those traits best align with the person you *should* be, not the person you want to be. Sometimes we want to be the type of person we can't realistically be.

> Your brand and culture only work if they are viewed as genuine. Projecting inauthenticity is a negative in the work environment and creates conflict in your culture.

"The journey of becoming a leader involves knowing what it is you do really well. Those will be the skills and capacities that are true for you and that you will be able to excel in. Being good at what you do allows you to prosper and become a leader people admire and want to work for.

"If you try to become a leader while being a person that you're not, people will instantly see through it. They'll see that you're uncomfortable in the role you're in. They'll see that you're not being authentic and eventually won't respect your position.

"Being an authentic leader means leveraging the things you're great at doing so you can excel. It also means that after you've been a leader for ten years, you still love what you're doing. Otherwise, if you don't like what you're doing, you'll be unsatisfied being a leader.

"I'm challenging you to engage in an exercise of self-knowledge, Jennifer. I want you to get clear about who you are, what you like, what you don't like, and what you're good at doing. How do you want the world to see you?"

As time begins to wind down in their session, Bill makes it clear that the responsibility for scheduling their meetings was Jennifer's. She would arrange sessions according to a rhythm and sequence that suited her, and Bill would make himself available.

FOLLOW-UP MEETING

A few weeks later, Jennifer reaches out and asks Bill if they can meet in his office. She doesn't want to be distracted during their conversation.

> It is the mentee's responsibility to establish the progression of meetings, but it is the mentor's responsibility to be flexible and accommodating to the request.

When they meet, Jennifer announces that she has identified three things she wants people to view as her brand.

"First and foremost, I want people to see that I am ethical," Jennifer says. "I want people to know that I have integrity. That's very important to me and to how I want to be viewed. I never want people to think that I make decisions for the wrong reasons."

"That's great, Jennifer," Bill says, "and it applies to the position you're already in. Even if you weren't interested in becoming a leader, it's a great life goal to have ethics and be seen as having integrity."

Jennifer continues, "I also want to be seen as caring about the greater good. My mission is to help the company and my boss be successful. I don't want to be the type of person who's always saying, 'Look at me!' I don't want the light shining on me. I want it to shine on the team. And if I know that I've contributed to the team, that's good enough for me.

"And the third thing is I want my brand to be someone who does a great job at work."

Bill replies, "Those are all very admirable. Let's walk through each one of them and see how you stack up. Let's start with people here at work. How do you think they view you today? And people you know outside of work? Do they think you have integrity and are ethical?"

Jennifer answers, "I believe I'm the kind of person about whom no one will ever say I didn't do my fair share. No one will say I cut corners. People know I'm a good person and am always willing to lend a hand. I like to think I'm viewed as someone who has ethics and integrity."

Bill goes on, "That's great that people view you that way, Jennifer. Let me ask you this: when you do something that you feel is cheating a bit or beating the system, how do you feel about it? Are you comfortable with that?"

Jennifer is quick to respond, "Oh no, I can't sleep at night if

I feel like I haven't done everything the right way. It bothers me and definitely causes me to have restless nights whenever I haven't done the best I could."

"That's great to hear. You have your guard up in your own mind for maintaining integrity and being ethical. That's wonderful, and it looks like we've covered your first and third goal. Let's move on to the second point you mentioned. Do you think people on your team, and outside of Flagler, too, view you as someone who doesn't want the light shining on you but rather on the greater good?"

"To be honest, not all the time," Jennifer admits. "There have been times when people got credit for the things that I worked on, and I complained about not getting recognition. I haven't always been the person I'd like to be. It bothers me when people get credit for things they didn't work on, especially when I know that I made a big contribution and didn't get any credit."

Bill acknowledges, "All right. It sounds like you'd like to be perceived a certain way, but you aren't projecting yourself that way. Let's look into it more. It seems to me like it doesn't bother you too much, because you continue to do it. Would you say that was true? You said, 'it happens,' not 'it happened one time.'"

"Yes, I see how I do that," Jennifer says. "I'll have to keep my eye on it. I admit that it doesn't overly bother me when I complain, but I know it's not how I should be reacting. Even though I know it's wrong, I keep doing it."

"Then that's an area you have to work on," Bill tells her. "If you want to change your brand, every time you feel the impulse to complain about not getting credit, you have to resist. Think about how you're responding physically. Try smiling when someone gets credit and you don't. Congratulate them. Take the high road in those situations.

"Is this something you feel you can do? If we fast-forward a year or two, do you think you'll still feel resentful, or do you think you'll be able to change your mindset and not let it bother you? Because if it's always going to bother you, we should find another trait to be your brand."

Jennifer takes a moment and then replies, "No, I already know when I'm doing it that it's not right. I just have to be more aware. I think this conversation will help me pay more attention in the future and catch myself."

"Remember, always take the high road. Compliment people. Don't express resentment, because you'll be seen

The mentor needs to feel comfortable in challenging the mentee, which can be uncomfortable but is an expectation.

in a way you don't want to be. We want your brand to be one that encourages individuals, regardless of whether they earned it or not. Believe me, Jennifer, I know it can be hard to do at times, but it will become a natural part of how you behave and will come more easily over time.

"We all struggle with this. When people get credit for things they didn't do, it goes against our desire to be truthful, doesn't it? I've had to deal with the same thing, and decided I wasn't going to let it bother me anymore. To be honest, when I let it go, I experienced less stress in my work life and knew my performance had improved. This is a great example of our internal culture clashing with our external brand. As in a business, it's an opportunity to enhance our culture, which, in turn, will improve our brand."

Jennifer acknowledges, "That's good to hear."

Bill continues, "When you see someone getting credit for something they didn't do, or even worse, that you did yourself, it comes up against your standards for integrity. But remember, you can only manage your own standards, not someone else's. You can't control what other people do. If someone got credit for something you worked on, you could mention it lightly when you have your next one-on-one meeting with the team leader without naming the person who did it. You can only take responsibility for your own integrity.

"Everything you mentioned, Jennifer, are traits for being a leader that people respect—being ethical, having integrity, helping your team, shining a light on others as well as offering congratulations. If that was your brand, who wouldn't want to work for you?

"The key points to keep in mind when building your personal brand and culture are:

- Think about how others see you;
- Select the qualities you have that you want to be known for;
- Review your alignment internally and externally with those qualities;
- Consider how you can change the way others view you, i.e., your brand and culture; and
- Identify what it is you need to do to get where you want to be and build your personal roadmap."

Chapter 2

---✸---

Speak Up: Gaining Confidence

A month goes by, and Jennifer is ready to meet again with Bill. She's been thinking about her brand and culture and how she wants to be seen by her colleagues at work. She sets up a breakfast meeting with Bill.

Normally when Jennifer shows up, she's upbeat and positive. She has a smile on her face and is engaged and excited during their meetings. This time, Bill notices that there's no smile and that she's slouching a bit.

Bill begins with some general questions and asks Jennifer how her week has been going. She answers curtly that everything is fine. He asks her what she'd like to discuss in their meeting. Again, her answers are short, and she seems distracted, even upset and confused.

Trying to figure out what's going on, Bill continues to probe gently. Bill and Jennifer have met only three times and are still getting to know each other, but Bill senses that something is not right. Jennifer is not forthcoming about whatever it is that is bothering her.

Bill goes on, "What are some of the positive things that have happened for you over the past month?"

Jennifer shares a few things about how she's worked on her brand. She rehashes some of their previous conversation, but there's no smile. Bill doesn't let her brush him off and continues to ask questions. As a mentor, it is Bill's job to help Jennifer become stronger. He can't take the easy route and let her carry on. He knows that in order to develop leadership in a person, sometimes you have to ask tough questions and go to a place that may not feel comfortable in order to make the relationship stronger. He presses on.

"Did you have any challenges in the last month?" Bill asks. "Tell me about something difficult that you had to deal with."

Jennifer is almost dismissive in her reply. Bill doesn't

give up. Even though her body language tells him that something is off, Jennifer doesn't avoid eye contact, so Bill knows that nothing is wrong in their relationship. She's simply not in a good mood, and Bill wants to know why.

Bill changes the subject and asks Jennifer if she did anything fun over the weekend. She tells Bill about a great movie she saw and the quality time she spent with her friends. While she's speaking, Jennifer becomes more animated and begins to smile. After chatting about Jennifer's social life, Bill goes back to the topic of work and asks if there is anything he can help her with.

"Has there been anything in the last couple of weeks that you feel I can help with?"

Part of the mentor's role is relationship building; part of the role of the mentee is to trust.

Finally, Jennifer opens up and says that she wishes people would listen to her more.

Bill knows they are finally getting somewhere. "Let me ask you one more question before I respond. Has there been a situation recently in which you felt people weren't listening to you?"

"Yes, in fact, there was," Jennifer offers. "We had a regular staff meeting earlier this week, and everything was fine. There was a lot of discussion in the room and, in all honesty, I didn't feel like I had anything to contribute, so I didn't say anything. After the meeting, my boss Rob came to me and asked me why I didn't participate.

"I told him that I didn't have anything to say and that I felt everybody was talking so much, mostly just to talk. Everything that needed to be said was said. Then Rob told me that he expected more from me. He wants me to be more engaged in our meetings. It upset me when he gave me the feedback."

Bill replies, "Jennifer, this happens all the time. I see it in meetings every day. There are always people who talk simply for the sake of talking. Someone will bring something valuable to a discussion and then the 'me-too' crowd repeats the same thing so that they can appear to be participating and adding value to the meeting. But all they are really doing is just taking up time in order to be heard. Some leaders like it and think it is active participation. A strong leader, though, will see it for what it is: someone reinforcing another person's opinion, which often creates an environment that discourages open dialogue. When people pile their views on top of one another's, it limits the opportunity to have a productive conversation of opposing opinions.

"Don't be discouraged, Jennifer. What strikes me as

important is that Rob came to you for more engagement. Why do you think he did that?"

Jennifer was silent. She was upset that Rob had challenged her to speak up more, but she hadn't thought about why he was doing it. Jennifer is still focused on not wanting to rehash an opinion that is already in the room.

Bill pauses and lets Jennifer think for a while. He wants to be sure that Jennifer understands why Rob is asking for her opinion.

After a few minutes, Jennifer says, "Maybe he's interested in something I have to say."

"I think that's it, Jennifer!" Bill exclaims. "I think Rob is asking you to engage more because he values your opinion. He didn't ask you to be involved in the meeting because he doesn't care what you have to say.

"You need to take it to heart, Jennifer, that Rob is coming to you for positive reasons. I know you felt like he was reprimanding you, but why would he come to you if you didn't have anything good to say? Rob knows you. I think Rob is coming to you to ask for your advice and for you to be more engaged because he wants to hear what you have to say. Does that make sense?"

After a brief pause, Bill continues, "This really has to do with your level of confidence. That's the challenge here. We need to focus on being confident in all situations.

"When you didn't get your promotion, you were upset because you believed you were the right person for the job. You had the confidence to reach out to me for mentoring, which demonstrates that you have confidence in yourself, but you may not always be expressing it. What Rob is saying is that he has confidence in you and wants you to act on it in meetings. But it seems that maybe you don't have confidence in yourself in certain situations, like in the recent staff meeting. So let's work on that.

"One of the key things in cultivating confidence is how you carry yourself. It goes back to our conversation about your personal brand and how people view you. You want to be viewed as someone who has confidence. Everyone wants to work for a leader whom they have confidence in. Many of us, myself included, have had leaders that we didn't believe in. You don't want to be that type of leader. You want to be a confident leader.

"Let's consider how you presented yourself in the staff meeting. Did you agree with everything that was said?"

Jennifer responds, "For the most part, I did. There were

a few points that I didn't 100 percent agree with, but I didn't think they were worth commenting about."

"Why not?" Bill asks, "If the goal of the meeting is to create value from the discussion and reach the best possible outcome? Let's say you are 90 percent in agreement with the results; that earns an A– score. How do we get to an A+ decision? Your contribution could have taken the outcome from 90 to 100 percent. But you didn't say anything because you thought there wasn't a big difference between 90 and 100 percent. You could have taken advantage of the situation by saying, 'I agree for the most part with what is being said, but I think there are a few details that could make things even better.' In that case, you wouldn't be agreeing 100 percent with what had already been said or be guilty of repeating other people's points of view. And you would not be interjecting a completely different perspective. You would be trying to improve the outcome.

"Do you want to give it a try? Are you willing to change your position and have the group see you in a different way?

"I think what will make a big difference for you, Jennifer, is your trying to see things in a new way. There's a difference between how you view a situation, how you experience it internally, and how others see it, whether in a meeting, a conversation, or an email exchange. If you have a differing opinion about something, you should articulate it with confidence. Let's work on you speaking out when you have something valuable to offer. Let's work on that."

Bill then explains that there are several behaviors Jennifer can adopt to convey confidence and proposes that they take a few minutes to discuss them. Then Jennifer can choose a few to work on over the course of the next month so that her coworkers begin to see her in a new light. Jennifer is pleased with the conversation they've been having and excited that she'll walk away with some concrete actions to put into practice.

BEHAVIORS FOR BUILDING CONFIDENCE

1. BE DECISIVE

The first behavior Bill discusses with Jennifer is being decisive. He encourages Jennifer to have an opinion.

"No one can take away your opinion, Jennifer. Don't be afraid to have a confident opinion, whether it's right or wrong. Even if you make a wrong decision, it's better than not taking a stand at all. A wrong decision can initiate a dialogue, which will help bring about a better group solution in the end. Even if you are unsure that you're right and what you are proposing turns out to be wrong, you will at least be seen as a decisive person. You should only state that you are uncertain or don't know something and want more information as a last resort.

"When you take a stand and are decisive, you will gain confidence in yourself. That's why I'm conveying this to you. It's not about being right or wrong. It's a way for you to develop confidence. Making a decision will give you confidence, even if someone else sees things differently. It's not as important how you articulate your position or whether your point of view was sufficiently broad to encompass the entire decision-making process. What matters is that you voiced your opinion, which you based on the information you had.

> Being decisive conveys a brand of engagement and confidence.

"As I already mentioned, people like working for a decisive leader. Think about your favorite political leader. Don't you agree that it's important that they come across as a decisive leader?"

"I may not like everything they say," Jennifer doesn't hesitate to respond, "but I do believe it's essential that they make decisions."

"Exactly," Bill goes on, "it's their job as the head of a state or a region to be decisive. But not everyone agrees with their decisions, right?"

"Of course not, Bill."

"That's why they got to where they are—not because they were always right, but because they were willing to make a decision and take a stand. That's how the process moves forward and how things improve. Political leaders are willing to make unpopular decisions so that the lives of their constituents change for the better. The same goes for you, Jennifer, when you make a decision. It may not always be popular, and it may not always be right, but you'll have made a decision and gained confidence every time. Decision making is not your enemy; it's your friend.

"When you make a decision as part of the team, not only do you gain confidence, but your team, too, becomes more decisive and better for it."

2. WORK WITH A CLEAR MIND

Bill moves on to the second behavior.

"Jennifer, when you're at work, what percentage of the day are you not distracted?"

Jennifer laughs and replies, "Bill, I'm distracted all day long! People are constantly calling, texting, and emailing me."

"I meant distraction that's not work-related, Jennifer," Bill clarifies. "How much of your time would you say are you engaged with things that don't have to do with work? Do you ever check social media? Do friends text you?"

"Oh, yeah," Jennifer answers, "off and on all through the day."

"Then how are you able to make decisions when you're constantly bombarded with information?"

"I grew up with technology and am good at it. I can handle information coming at me in all kinds of ways," Jennifer explains.

Bill concurs, "I don't doubt it. I bet you do a great job, but, Jennifer, what if you had a clear mind? Do you think you'd be able to improve your decision-making ability and increase your confidence, even slightly?"

"For sure, it's hard at times when I'm trying to have a conversation with someone and my phone's going off, I'm getting texts, and emails are coming in. I have to admit it's very distracting."

"I'll tell you what," Bill advises. "I encourage you to do what I do. Every day, I block out periods of time on my calendar—the first and last hours of the day and the hour after lunch—and I make sure that I use at least two of them every day. I use the time to focus on various tactical tasks, like clearing out my inbox and responding to people who are waiting to hear from me. Whatever it is, I don't check my phone, and I don't let people interrupt me. The goal of this time is to eliminate distractions from the rest of the day. When I am in meetings or working on strategic initiatives, I don't want tactical items cluttering up my mind.

"I treat that blocked time as a gift. I'm able to focus on specific tasks, which allows me to be better at my job. In a way, it's like practicing before going onstage. It enables me to clear my head, because I've taken care of the emails in my inbox and am not worrying about them anymore. Then when I'm interacting with a colleague, having a phone conversation, or making a presentation, I'm fully present. I encourage everyone who works with me to do the same thing."

3. STAY FOCUSED

"Because it's so easy to lose focus during meetings and miss part of the discussion, I never keep my laptop open or my phone out. I try to have as few distractions as possible when I'm in a meeting. Every person is different, so find out what works best for you so that you can be present and focused.

"Learning to stay focused is like flexing a muscle. Whether you're in a meeting or a one-on-one conversation with someone, it's an opportunity to present your brand and demonstrate who you are. The more focused you are, the better you will be, just like the athlete who has trained for an event and is now giving it his all.

> Every interaction is an opportunity to demonstrate your brand and your strengths. Take advantage of every phone call, email, or meeting to present yourself fully.

"It may be that you shouldn't even be in certain meetings. Everyone fears missing out, whether by missing a meeting that one was invited to or by setting up a meeting and leaving someone out. In all companies, people go to meetings they don't need to attend. I encourage you not to be afraid of declining a meeting invitation. If you feel it isn't necessary to attend, have the confidence to say no and use your energy in a more productive way."

4. FOLLOW THROUGH

Bill continues, "The best way to enhance your brand, your culture, and your confidence all at the same time is to do what you say you are going to do. Follow through.

"We are all pleasantly surprised whenever someone does what they promised, whether in a restaurant, on the phone, or at a store. We gain confidence and respect the person who was honest with us.

"At work, people want the same thing. When you keep your word, people will view you as someone they can count on. As a leader, you want people to respect you and be able to rely on you, even if you have to change their expectations from time to time. If you promised a report by a certain date and are unable to meet the deadline for whatever reason, communicate the delay. A reasonable person will respect that, even though sometimes there may be no possibility of flexibility. Be secure in yourself and state when something is going off track and how you're going to rectify the situation. That is all part of following through and how people will gain confidence in your leadership."

5. BE RESPECTFUL OF THE CONTEXT

"Earlier you mentioned that you don't like it when people speak out in meetings and don't have anything meaningful to contribute. You lose respect for them in those situations. I'd like you to think about finding the balance between speaking when you have something to say and not speaking in order to avoid saying something merely to say it. It's like learning to walk a tightrope; you need balance.

"We have to learn to be respectful of the situation we find ourselves in and find the line between saying something that adds value to the conversation and speaking for the sake of speaking. Rob came to you asking for more engagement because he thought you had something to offer, not to hear you speak. It's challenging to walk this fine line."

PUTTING IT ALL INTO PRACTICE

"Bill, that all sounds great in theory," Jennifer responds, "but I'd like some practical tips. How do I find balance and gain confidence in the group decision-making process? Can you give me something concrete I can do when I find myself in these situations?"

"That's a great question," Bill answers. "Let me ask you a question before we go on. When you were growing up, did you play any sports? Did you dance or do anything like that?"

"Yeah, I was an accomplished dancer all through school,"

Jennifer replies. "I also played some softball and swam, but my favorite activity was dancing."

Bill continues, "Jennifer, when you were dancing, especially if you were dancing with a partner or tap dancing, did you ever feel like things were moving too fast and you wanted to slow things down?"

"You must have been a dancer, Bill!" Jennifer exclaims.

Bill jokes, "I've never danced in my life, but it sounds like something a dancer would do."

Jennifer jumps in, "Absolutely! When I did ballet, I danced with a partner and had to slow everything down in my mind because there was so much choreography going on between us. If I didn't slow things down, I'd get ahead of myself and make mistakes."

"That's interesting," Bill says. "I used to play a lot of baseball. One of the things I had a hard time with as I came up against better and better pitchers was my ability to hit fast-moving balls. When an off-speed pitch would come at me, I'd have a hard time hitting it. What I tried to do—and what I knew all great hitters do—was to slow down the ball while it was coming toward me. Even though the pitches weren't nearly as fast as those in the major leagues, I was a kid, and they were fast to me. I had to slow everything down so I could hit the ball. It helped me a lot as a hitter. It sounds like you had to do the same thing when you were dancing.

"I did it through repetitions and lots of batting practice. I became used to the movement of the ball, which allowed me to slow the ball down mentally. The practice and the mindset clearly helped. Knowing you were a dancer, I'm sure you had many hours of practice to get to the same place."

"Yes, I did," Jennifer confirms. "You're right, but what does this have to do with work?"

"It has everything to do with work," Bill assures her. "Think about when you were in the staff meeting, and everyone was talking. You were paying attention to some degree, but you were also looking at your phone or maybe thinking about other things. A lot was going on for you. It's easy to get overwhelmed in a situation like that. What I do when I'm in a similar situation is to try and slow everything down, just like you did when you were dancing with a partner or like I did when I was trying to hit a curve ball.

"I do the same thing at work. I try to slow down all the information that's coming at me so that I can make good decisions—ones that are not rushed, not made under pressure, and not thought through sufficiently. I obtained this skill through repetition and staying aware of slowing my thoughts down and not rushing to conclusions."

"When you were dancing, you were under pressure to execute flawlessly with your partner, so you slowed things down to minimize errors. Similarly, when you're in a meeting and everything is happening at once, it gets overwhelming. If you can slow down the process, you'll be able to think things through and provide better responses.

"Jennifer, when you were dancing with your partner, were you really slowing things down? Did you start dancing slowly?"

"No, not really," Jennifer says, "but in my mind, I was."

"Exactly! That's my point," Bill elaborates. "You want to slow things down in the same way when you're in a meeting. No one will know, of course, what you're doing, just like your partner and the audience didn't know that you were slowing down the dancing in your head. It looked like you were dancing beautifully. The same holds true when you're working with a colleague, making decisions, or speaking in a meeting.

"Often when I'm speaking, in my mind, I slow the words that are coming out of my mouth. In reality, I'm speaking normally, but it enables me to concentrate on what I'm saying. I execute better and don't get overwhelmed. It helps me tremendously.

"When I first started doing this, I was afraid I would lose my connection with whomever I was talking to or that I would be slow to respond. Once I realized that wasn't going to happen, I saw that I was able to reduce the external forces that were creating pressure on me to make a decision or say something I didn't mean.

"Jennifer, it takes maturity to do this. It's not something that you'll be able to do overnight. It'll take practice to learn to slow down the process and focus," Bill clarifies. "Is there anything you'd like to ask to me?"

"You've given me so much today," Jennifer declares. "I want to put it into practice. What do you think I should focus on?"

"Here's what I propose," Bill says. "At your next staff meeting, set for yourself the goal of making two key contributions. You don't have to set the world on fire; just contribute twice in the meeting. For example, you could take responsibility for following up on a particular action item. It could be that simple. There are always action items in every meeting, and you could be sure to walk away with at least one of them.

"You could also offer an insight or give feedback based on something you observed out in the field. You're a project manager who works with a wide range of initiatives. Bring something to the group that you've noticed that could bring value to the meeting. If you're able to do more, great, but let's count on you offering at least two contributions to the meeting."

> Mentally slowing down decision making improves results.

"I can definitely do that. I was expecting something a lot harder."

Bill reminds her, "Remember to slow it down when you're in the meeting. Think of yourself as being on stage, like when you were dancing. Always remember that you're on stage at work and to slow things down."

A FEW WEEKS LATER

A few weeks after their coaching session, Bill and Jennifer run into each other in the parking lot. Bill immediately asks, "So, how's it going? Have you been able to practice some of the things we talked about?"

"Yes," Jennifer reports, "I'm happy to say that we had our regular staff meeting yesterday, and it went well. At first, I was afraid and intimidated because I was putting so much pressure on myself."

"That's normal," Bill acknowledges. "Whenever we try something new, it's natural that we're going to feel more pressure."

"But I didn't let it stop me," Jennifer goes on. "There was talk of an initiative that was similar to something I'd dealt with the previous day with one of my internal customers, and I felt I should share it with the group. As I was talking, I noticed at one point that people were leaning in to listen. I could see it in their body language. I also saw that some people were smiling and shaking their heads in agreement. I knew that what I was saying was landing and making a difference. It felt great!"

Bill listens closely. "Let me ask one thing, Jennifer. What did you gain from that experience?"

"I gained confidence," Jennifer says without hesitation. "I started smiling, too. They welcomed what I had to say, which gave me the courage to add more. The more they leaned in, the more I wanted to share."

"Jennifer, that's it! That's what it's all about," Bill exclaims. "You did your dance and got a standing ovation. You learned four things:

- Contribute so you gain confidence and, more importantly, so people gain confidence in you.
- Slow the process down in your mind, not in reality.
- Give the best that you have; it's all that we can ever do in life.
- Be confident in your decision to add value to the conversation; if you're not, others won't be either.

"You fulfilled the assignment, Jennifer, and reaped the rewards. Congratulations!"

Chapter 3

---------- ✳ ----------

Get Involved: Social Growth Outside the Workplace

When Jennifer gets in touch with Bill for her next mentoring session, Bill is traveling. Rather than let too much time pass, they decide to meet over the phone. Bill is in his hotel room in California and Jennifer is in the office when they have their call.

Bill and Jennifer's relationship has continued to develop since their last meeting when Jennifer was reluctant to share her frustrations with Bill. After chatting briefly about Jennifer's life outside of work, Bill asks, "Last month when we got together, you were frustrated because you felt Rob was giving you a hard time about not engaging in staff meetings. How's it been going since we ran into each other in the parking lot, when you shared with me that you spoke up in the staff meeting?"

Jennifer replies, "I think I'm doing great and gaining confidence. Like you said, what's important is how I feel internally and what I show to the outside world. I think others are changing their perception of me and starting to see me as a confident person. I'm feeling a whole lot better about myself, but now I have a new problem. I really want to be promoted, but in my current role, there's no opportunity for helping others. I'm more certain now than ever that I would make a great leader, but there are no openings. Now that I am gaining self-confidence, I feel frustrated because I'm ready to move into leadership and nothing's available.

"I've been having a lot of sleepless nights lately, thinking it might be time for me to leave Flagler. Maybe I even need to change the type of work I do. I'm eager to move into a leadership role and don't want my company to stand in the way. That's how I'm feeling, and I'm not sure what to do. I don't want to lose any more sleep over it and am hoping you can help."

Bill says, "Okay, I guess we really did do a good job improving your self-confidence! You've taken it so far that now you're having an adrenaline rush. That's great, but we also want to manage your confidence and not have it turn into arrogance. No one likes an arrogant person. There's a fine line between confidence and arrogance.

"You've established yourself at Flagler and are well respected. You and your leader, Rob, have a good relationship. You're lucky to have the kind of job that involves managing projects for other departments. Your role naturally creates a way for lots of people outside of your team to know who you are, which boosts your brand and culture within the company. You're definitely heading in the right direction with the things we've been talking about—your brand and culture along with your confidence—and I think being at Flagler has something to do with it.

"Speaking about changing jobs, when was the last time you were at the grocery store, Jennifer, and there was a long line? Did you stay in the line that you were in?"

"I am not sure what this has to do with changing jobs, but I probably did change lines a couple of times. I get annoyed if I'm in a line that isn't moving," Jennifer admits.

"And when you got to the register, do you think switching lines helped you get there any faster?"

"To be honest, no. Many times, the original line got to the register faster."

Bill sympathizes, "We all do that when we're anxious to move forward, and then we end up in the slow lane. I think if you left Flagler now, it would be like switching lines in the grocery store. I'd like to encourage you to stay here for a while longer and see where it takes you. I think there's a good chance it will get you to the cash register a lot faster. If after a few years, you feel that you've done everything you can and still have the desire to move on, that will be different. I've only been mentoring you a few months. I'm glad you're confident, but I'd also like you to be patient and see if something develops here at Flagler."

Bill continues, "Let me share an example in which we in leadership failed in this type of situation. It will give you an understanding of what it's like from the other side.

"Several years ago, an operations manager left the firm, and the position became available. We posted the job internally because we wanted to give a person already in the company a chance to move into the role. The number one performer on the operations team applied and, based on his great work ethic and experience, we promoted him. We did know the individual had no prior management experience, though it was clear he was eager for the promotion.

"Within two weeks, we all knew it was a bad decision, including the new manager. We made multiple mistakes in the hiring process, such as not providing the employee with any previous mentoring, relying on day-to-day performance as the key driver in our decision, and believing that his eagerness and desire was sufficient. On top of that, we had a relatively light management development program, so we didn't have the tools to help this new manager grow professionally. Within six months, we had to move him back into operations, where he is still excelling today, which is why I don't want to mention his name. Some people are just not built to be managers.

"This scenario demonstrates why mentoring is key—it allows leadership to evaluate people through meaningful interactions. Just as importantly, it allows mentees to see if leadership is right for them and if they're ready for it."

Bill had stuck a pin in Jennifer's balloon of excitement. She responds, "Do you think I'm not ready? You sound like you're not confident that I can lead."

In an effort to create reassurance, Bill gives confidence in his feedback. "I think you're heading in the right direction and are showing the skills to provide leadership. The point of sharing the story is to emphasize that leadership requires ongoing development. Personally, I welcome our mentoring sessions because they allow me to hone my leadership craft. In the story I shared with you, we leaders didn't invest enough in the individual to help him become ready. We all need to grow in our leadership journey, and you're on your way."

"Here's what I suggest. Continue with the energy you have for the areas we've been working on and start leveraging it in your social growth."

Bill pauses for a moment.

Jennifer is puzzled. "Social growth? What am I supposed to do with that? Do you mean make more friends? That doesn't make any sense to me."

"No, that's not what I mean," Bill answers. "I'm not talking about social networking, and I'm not talking about personal growth either. I care about you developing into a better leader, and by social growth I mean taking the traits and practices of leadership and applying them to areas outside of work."

"I kind of get the idea of social growth, but I don't really understand what you mean," Jennifer responds.

"Social growth has to do with involvement outside of the workplace. Of course, that involvement can mean different things to different people. When you think of getting involved outside of work, what does it mean for you, Jennifer?"

"My first thought is getting involved with my church or local community, or a nonprofit that I like," Jennifer replies.

> Social growth should be viewed as professional development outside the workplace.

"Absolutely, Jennifer, those are great areas for developing social growth," Bill says. "Another area that you might want to consider is something to do with project management since you're a project manager. There must be a professional project management association that you could get involved with. Or there may be a nonprofit organization that would benefit from your project management experience and welcome your help. I suggest exploring opportunities like that. Maybe you could expand your breadth of skills while helping your local community at the same time."

Jennifer says, "That all sounds nice and valuable, and would definitely make me feel like I'm a better person, but how is it going to help me become a leader at Flagler?"

"It's simple," Bill elaborates. "If there's an opportunity for you to provide leadership and practice being a leader outside of the walls of Flagler, you will grow professionally. And that's what counts. That's why it's called social *growth*. It will enable you to practice your skills before embarking on a leadership role here at Flagler. Second, you'll have a chance to build a network of individuals who could potentially mentor you one day or the reverse, people whom you could mentor in the future. And last but not least, another beautiful thing about social growth is the intrinsic value it offers, knowing that you're helping others while also helping yourself."

A developing leader needs simulated opportunities for leadership, which social growth outside of the work environment can provide.

"Okay, I get it. I like what you're saying, but where do I begin? There are so many options. Plus, Flagler sponsors a community outreach program. I'm often overwhelmed by all the possibilities I read about in the emails they send out."

"Flagler's program is a great way to start your search. We're lucky to work for a company that offers community outreach. You could also go to any local coffee shop and check their bulletin board for notices from organizations looking for help. Or go online and search what's available in your neighborhood. What it boils down to is finding a situation that you value. If you're investing your time to grow socially and professionally, you want to make sure to do it in way that you feel rewards your efforts.

"One approach, as I mentioned, is to volunteer your project management expertise. That's a great way to go. Perhaps there's a local program for youths or seniors. Would you like doing something like that? To me, the most important thing, in addition to gaining leadership experience, is that you're doing something you enjoy. That's the first thing to determine, and I can't help with that. When I brought this up, what was the first thing that came to your mind?"

"Getting involved with seniors popped into my head," Jennifer answers. "I think I'd enjoy that. My parents live on the other side of the country, and I don't get to see them as much as I'd like. I miss those parental relationships."

"Excellent. That seems like an easy thing to do. There are plenty of programs for seniors, whether through the YMCA or a senior center near where you live. Why don't you look into that?

"I also encourage you to look for a professional project management organization, which would be great for developing your networking relationships. Having a network of professionals is so valuable. It could include friends you went to school with or, perhaps, people who left Flagler and are now working for other companies. What I'm suggesting is not the type of friend you'd go to the movies with or out to dinner, but someone you could meet for a cup of coffee to talk about challenges at work or other things going on professionally. Who knows, you could even find yourself providing mentorship to a colleague!"

> As mentees gain confidence, they should look for opportunities to lead through charity or community efforts or by becoming mentors.

"Of course, Bill," Jennifer says, "that seems so obvious. I should have been doing more of that already."

Bill continues, "It's a muscle that we all have to learn to flex, and it takes effort. Often when we get together with our professional friends, we complain about work or gossip, but the real value in those relationships is to have meaningful conversations with people who share our professional goals."

Jennifer asks, "Can you tell me about your experience? Have you gone through anything similar?"

"How do you think I got to Flagler?" he answers.

"What do you mean?"

"I'm here at Flagler precisely because of a type of situation that I'm encouraging you to pursue."

"Can you tell me the story?" Jennifer persists.

"Sure. Many years ago," Bill relates, "I had a friend who worked for me at another company. His name is Steve. When he left the company, I was sad to see him go, but he asked if we could meet for coffee in the mornings from time to time. It worked out great because Steve's new job was right around the corner from where I live. Every two to three months, we'd meet, and over time we developed a relationship similar to what you and I are creating.

"Steve and I always sat in the same spot outside a café, and when Steve's new boss Ashley walked by, she would say hello. Eventually, I got to know Ashley, too. One day she asked me to get a cup of coffee with her, and I started meeting regularly with Ashley, too. Every few weeks I'd leave home thirty minutes early to grab a cup of coffee with one of the two of them.

"Once, when Ashley and I met, she told me that they really needed someone like me at the firm where she and Steve worked, which turned out to be Flagler. I didn't know much about Flagler at the time, which was over ten years ago. We were a much smaller company back then.

"I was flattered that Ashley felt I had the experience that was needed at Flagler. I had taken the time to get to know Ashley and was impressed by what she was doing. She headed up technology, and I had been head of finance at my former employer. We started having conversations about my eventual move to Flagler, and that's how I ended up here.

"It was as easy as that: someone who had worked for me wanted a mentor and, in turn, connected me to one of his colleagues who also wanted to build a relationship with me, and she eventually introduced me to Flagler. I've been with Flagler ever since, and it was one of the best career moves I ever made. All I did was put myself out there. When someone asked for help, I said yes and then put effort into the relationship. I didn't go into it expecting I'd get something out of it for myself. Honestly the only thing I was interested in was building and maintaining friendships."

"Wow, that's a great story. I'm impressed!"

"In the end, Jennifer, the important thing is I was genuine in those relationships. My only goal was to build relationships. When you go into it with the right spirit, good things can come of it. For you, though, the purpose is to practice mentoring. Maybe the people you'll meet will be able to help you down the road, but your motivation has to be genuine. You truly have to want to help."

Jennifer agrees, "I love that. It's helpful. So how exactly should I go about this? Do you have any actionable items I can take away?"

"The first thing to do is to find a community-oriented or professional organization that you want to participate in. Pick only one for now to stick your toe in the water. You may not feel there's a good connection, or it may become too much to handle. Bear in mind that if it's not a good fit, you can always move on.

"If it turns out to be a good first date, then go on a second date. If it's a bad first date, end it right there. You haven't committed yourself to anything. Your goal is to gain new experiences and grow your leadership foundation. Find something that you have a passion for. Most people won't engage in extracurricular activities unless they enjoy it.

Remember you're in charge. Take your time to find a good situation, one that works for you, but don't put it ahead of your job. You're doing this to make yourself better at work, so be sure to keep your priorities in order.

"Lastly, Jennifer, if you know someone outside of Flagler or a colleague you've worked with in the past, start meeting with him or her on a regular basis. Don't force it. Grab lunch or a coffee together for now and engage in honest, work-related conversations. Start with one person and see how it goes. It's a great way to extend yourself without overcommitting."

ABOUT A MONTH LATER

A month goes by, and Bill hasn't heard anything from Jennifer. Then, he receives a text from her asking if they can meet for coffee. Bill thinks that he's probably become one of the people on her coffee circuit. The following week, Bill and Jennifer meet at the coffee shop near their office.

First thing Bill asks, "Am I your first coffee connection or have you met with others?"

"I've actually reached out to a couple of people," Jennifer reports, "and we've met for coffee. Like you said, mornings are good, so we can keep chatting if things are going well, or make it quick if not, and head to work."

"You're right." Then Bill asks if she's joined any organizations.

"I did," she carries on. "Joining the local project managers' association made the most sense to me. I felt that would be a good way to meet people who do the same thing I do. If nothing else, I figured I could get better at my day-to-day job and find out what goes on in other companies. I've learned that my struggles and challenges aren't unique and are genuinely real.

"I really enjoyed the first meeting I attended and met a few people I can call if I have a problem at work. I'm looking forward to seeing where those relationships go."

"Anything more?" Bill asks. "Are there other things you want to do?"

Jennifer responds, "I believe I have the time to do more, but I didn't want to over-extend myself."

"Here's something simple you can do," Bill suggests. "As you mentioned, Flagler regularly sends out community awareness emails. Why don't you keep an eye out for a once-a-year event, like a walk-a-thon, a lake cleanup, or a Habitat for Humanity project—something you can do once to see if you like it. It will be an opportunity for you to meet other people and see if it's something you're interested in getting more involved with later on."

"Great idea, Bill!"

"The one concern I have is that your efforts in social growth don't become all-consuming. Remember, you're volunteering, and you don't want to create more stress for yourself, whether it's professionally motivated or community-minded.

"Learn from my experience. Once I had to confront this precise issue. I was involved with two local financial organizations, coached my kids in sports, was the president of one of my kid's youth organizations, and ran the local YMCA. I woke up one day and realized that my community involvement was distracting me from my real work at the office and from my family. I ended up having to resign from some roles and, to be honest, I felt like I had failed. But I realized how important it was to keep my priorities in order. This experience helped me to learn to say no to these situations with the focus of not overcommitting.

"Before we head back to the office, Jennifer, let me remind you of a few key points:

- Seek outside activities related to your professional or personal interests that will make you a better person.
- Keep an open mind as you meet people; they may be able to help you grow professionally and personally; you never know who you'll meet.

- Your brand and confidence will benefit as your peers at work recognize your community outreach.
- Make sure you maintain balance, and don't overextend yourself."

Chapter 4

---�֍---

Give and Serve:
Influencing Others

A month goes by, and Jennifer reaches out to Bill for their regular check-in meeting. They decide to have lunch at the diner across the street from the office. Bill assumes all's been going well for Jennifer since he hasn't heard from her since they last got together.

After a short conversation about some traveling Jennifer has been doing, Bill hears that things are progressing well with the project management organization. Jennifer speaks positively about it and seems satisfied with what she's doing. Bill is encouraged that Jennifer is on the right track.

Bill asks how she's doing with some of the other things

she's working on. Jennifer shares how comfortable she's been feeling in staff meetings. She participates regularly and has no reservations about contributing her opinions. She mentions she feels like she's getting her time at bat that they had discussed previously. The best part is that her manager has been giving her positive feedback, and not just with regard to her engagement in meetings. He's pleased with her overall performance and has given her more challenging projects to work on.

Jennifer's volunteering efforts have also been going great. She doesn't feel overcommitted and has resisted the desire to do more, remembering Bill's advice not to overdo volunteering in order to continue enjoying it. The most reassuring development, however, for Jennifer is that her peers, both on her team and from other teams she works with, have started asking her for advice on a range of topics. Her brand is going in the direction she wants.

Bill uses this as an opportunity to announce that Jennifer is becoming an influencer. Judging from the expression on her face, it's not a word she would have ever applied to herself.

Bill elaborates, "You're getting praise from your boss about the quality of your work and receiving good assignments. Your peers are coming to you for advice, and you're finding satisfaction in activities outside of your job. Doesn't that feel like a springboard for success?"

Jennifer pauses for a moment and says, "Yes, I do feel that's true, but why do you say I'm an influencer?"

"The big thing for me was when I heard you say that peers outside of your department are coming to you to ask for advice. It sounds like you're doing an effective job of influencing them without even trying, and that is the key to being a good influencer."

Jennifer's response is one of surprise, which encourages Bill to continue. "There are three basic areas in which influencing takes place. First is in daily interactions. We are either being influenced or influencing others during our daily exchanges with people. Everything you do affects the way you influence, whether it's how you articulate what you're saying or how you carry yourself, and all of it relates to your culture and your brand.

"When you're proud of your brand, people will notice. To repeat what we've already talked about, think of yourself as an actress on stage, and everyone is watching you. Present yourself in the best way possible. But I want to be clear: that doesn't mean you're acting when you're at work. Always be yourself and take pride in the fact that people are watching you. It's not something to be afraid of.

> The goal is always to present your best self. It will naturally elevate your brand.

"Another thing to bear in mind is that influencing is good practice for becoming a leader. You could think of it as doing repetitions when exercising with the goal of building strength.

"Influencing happens in 360 degrees, in all directions at once, which is what most people who aren't in leadership positions would love to be able to do. Of course, what's even more exciting is to influence people who aren't part of your natural peer group."

Bill suggests, "Let's use our relationship as an example. How are you influencing me?"

Jennifer realizes that she doesn't see her relationship with Bill in this way, but she responds. "I never thought of it quite that way, but I guess I am giving you an at-bat in leadership, a chance to use your experiences to help me grow professionally. Plus, it gives you new opportunities to exercise your leadership skills."

Bill likes where the discussion is headed, but Jennifer still doesn't realize that she is influencing Bill.

"Great answer, and I would say you are correct. But you only looked at half of the equation. You're influencing me, too. Along with a vision of your career goals, you give me the fresh perspective of someone with different challenges from another department. You influence me through your views and ideas."

Jennifer smiles with a sense of accomplishment. "I never thought of it that way. Clearly, I wasn't trying to influence you; it simply happened. But to be honest, you have to be open-minded to being influenced, like I am in these meetings."

"Agreed. I go into our sessions with an open mind. Now let's think about other ways you could exert influence. Perhaps you could impact team leaders or the project managers at the professional association you're involved with or even some of Flagler's external vendors. Any of those groups of people would provide excellent opportunities for influencing."

> Both the mentor and the mentee should grow in the relationship. Growth is not one-sided in mentoring.

Jennifer starts to have a strange look on her face, and Bill wonders what's concerning her.

Jennifer begins, "I didn't intend for this to lead to influencing. I don't want to feel that I'm affecting how people behave. That feels political to me, and I'm not a political person."

"You're right about that," Bill agrees. "Generally speaking, one of the worst things anyone can say about an organization is that it's political. The word has many negative connotations, and at work, politics is not something most people want to align themselves with.

"When I speak about being an influencer, I'm referring to honesty and trustworthiness. That's how you influence people. When you influence others, you're trying to help them be the best they can be. You're not trying to get them to do what you want them to do."

THE ART OF LEADERSHIP INFLUENCE

"Influencing is a delicate thing. Many people think influencing means getting others to do what they say. I'm talking about a very different type of influencing. I like to think of it as leadership influence, and it requires being honest and trustworthy and building relationships so that you can help others grow and succeed. How can you help others learn from the journey you've already taken?

"Think of our relationship, Jennifer. I'm not trying to get

you to do what I want you to do. I'm trying to help you be the best person that you can be, but it is a form of influencing. I'm trying to help you so that you become a great leader. A leader who's an influencer is a person who is genuinely focusing on what's best for the people he works with, the company, and their customers. The purpose is always the greater good, not oneself.

"Jennifer, we've already talked about how you're viewed by the outside world and that it's up to you to define how that will be. You determine whether you're someone who's viewed as political or authentic. Either you're trying to help people be better at what they do, or you're not. It's your decision. I'm assuming you want to be viewed as genuine because you reached out to me and because of the traits I've seen in you since we started getting to know each other."

> Influence comes from a desire for excellence. It should feel like a natural response.

"True," Jennifer acknowledges. "I like everything you're saying. It fits with the other things we've talked about, but can you give me an example? Have you known someone who was a good influencer and then became a leader?"

Bill thinks for a minute and says, "I can think of several examples, but there is one from several years ago which is a great success story and similar to your situation. In fact, Kelsey was just like you at one time. She's on our team over in finance.

"Kelsey was a strong performer who wanted to move into leadership. She felt it was the next step in her journey, but she had no leadership experience, nor a mentor.

"Kelsey had interviewed multiple times for a managerial position. Everyone thought she was a star in the organization, but she never succeeded in becoming a manager. She'd go through the interviewing process and once made it to the final round, but she was never chosen to be a manager.

"After the first set of interviews, word on the street was that Kelsey's performance was stagnating and that she was looking to leave Flagler. In situations when people want growth and don't get it, they often look elsewhere and lose interest in their current role.

"Then, something changed in Kelsey, and her drive returned. She continued to pursue her goal. Each time she wasn't promoted, she'd come to those of us who had interviewed her and asked for feedback. She wanted to know what she could do to be better.

"Right then, we all knew that this was an individual who

was genuine in her desire to grow and was taking the time to invest in herself. Shortly after she lost the job the second time, Kelsey's persona completely changed. She started to conduct herself like a natural leader. Specifically, when her immediate supervisor, Dan, was going out of town, Kelsey reached out to him to ask if she could run the staff meeting while he was away instead of having to cancel the meeting.

"The way she presented it to Dan was that she wanted an opportunity to learn how to run a meeting, and what better way to do it than to fill in while he was out of town. She didn't say that she wanted to replace him, but rather, she explained that it was a chance for her to better herself while, at the same time, helping out Dan and the team.

"Dan let her do it. The feedback from the team was that the meeting went great and that her style for running it was effective. Kelsey did such a great job running the staff meetings that Dan decided to let her do it regularly, even when he was there.

"Not long after that, the team was conducting job interviews, and Kelsey asked Dan if she could be part of the process. Her pitch to Dan was that having someone from the finance team participate in the interviews would give the candidates an opportunity to ask questions about the work environment and determine if it was a good fit.

"Twice she'd asked for an opportunity to develop. Soon, she was influencing her team, becoming a voice for Dan, and meeting job candidates. She grew professionally while still reporting to Dan.

"Fast forward. Dan got a promotion, and his position became available. Kelsey figured that since she'd already applied twice, she might as well apply again. This time, she went into the interviews knowing that she could lead. She'd had experience interviewing job candidates and had led staff meetings, and she was aware that she was influencing her team. She had trained by going through many repetitions of leadership, so it was easier for her to progress to a management role. By all accounts, she's doing a great in her new role. It took Kelsey over a year to grow into a leader before she actually became one."

Jennifer is clearly impressed.

Bill asks Jennifer if she would like to meet Kelsey. "I'd be happy to introduce you. Maybe the two of you could go for lunch. She works over in my building, and I'm sure she'd enjoy the opportunity to help someone like you achieve the same thing she did."

Jennifer is enthusiastic. "How could I not want to meet her? Kelsey sounds like she'd be a great role model for me. I'd love to get together with her and hear her thoughts on how she achieved her goals."

"Before we run out of time, I want to encourage you to do one more thing before we meet again. I'd like you to identify at least one person, maybe two, that you feel you can proactively influence, and it has to be genuine. Your mission is to find the next Jennifer. Don't expect to get anything out of it other than supporting someone to be the best he or she can be. That's your assignment. Find the right person, and when we get back together, I'll be eager to hear how it goes."

SIX WEEKS LATER

Bill begins to wonder why he hasn't heard anything from Jennifer. Then they run into each other at an all-company meeting. When the meeting ends, Bill and Jennifer take some time to catch up. Bill wants to hear how things have been going.

One of the most exciting things Jennifer has to share is that the perfect opportunity fell into her lap. A new person at Flagler, Michael, joined Jennifer's team, and Jennifer proactively reached out to him. Michael didn't know the team members, didn't know how things were done at Flagler, and, most importantly, didn't know what it was like to work for their boss, Rob.

Jennifer relates the story to Bill. "I told Michael that I had worked for Rob for a while and would be happy to share with him what it was like. I especially wanted him to know about Rob's legendary one-on-one meetings that he likes to have with each of us team members every two to three weeks. He has his own style for going over what we're working on, so I suggested to Michael that we do some role-playing. I knew I'd be able to give him some good pointers. I want to continue being the go-to person for Michael."

Bill thinks they're done talking when Jennifer adds, "And something else came up that's even better. I've been asked to serve on the project management review committee and help establish a new set of protocols. I never dreamed I'd be recommended by my team members! It's a unique opportunity to be involved with my peers from other departments and help set a new direction for how we work as project managers."

"That's great," Bill congratulates Jennifer. "It's a terrific opportunity! And think about this. You were recommended by your team and Rob to be on the committee, which means not only are you influencing them, but they're giving you a chance to be influenced by others and an opportunity to grow professionally. Influencing is not one-directional. It goes both ways. You are creating your own allies and supporters as much as you're supporting others as an influencer. Think of Kelsey. She cultivated supporters at the same time that she was working for Dan.

"The key thing to remember when influencing is that it refers back to what you want your personal brand and culture to be. Your brand and culture are the foundation. They determine the type of influencer you will be and how you express your leadership capabilities. Every great leader is an influencer first.

"Until we see each other again, keep in mind that when you're influencing:

· You're highlighting your personal brand and culture;
· You're always genuine because people know when you're not; and
· You're building a network of peers who are your allies."

Chapter 5

———— ✳ ————

Accept Responsibility: Managing Your Direct Reports

It's been over a year that Bill and Jennifer have been working together. During that time, Jennifer has gone through periods of highs and lows. The most challenging situation occurred when Jennifer was recruited by a local firm and was on the verge of leaving Flagler. Jennifer saw the opportunity as a potential for a quick promotion to leadership. She was initially excited by the idea of a fresh start. At the same time, she was drawn to staying at Flagler for the relationships she had built and the satisfaction of knowing she was doing a great job.

Eventually, Jennifer made the decision to stay, and she

learned a lesson about the value of building personal capital. She'd been tested—she'd gone through the recruiting process and realized her situation at Flagler was better than she had thought. Her personal relationships and brand she was creating internally was worth more than she had realized. In all, she found the experience rewarding. It left her with a renewed feeling of confidence.

We all deal with similar dynamics in relationships, whether at work or in our personal lives. We become relaxed in a relationship until a challenge suddenly occurs. Then the tension rises, which in Jennifer's case was about leaving. It's at that point when we discover the value, or lack thereof, of the relationship. Often, we need a test to validate the worth of a relationship. For Jennifer, the test was priceless and necessary.

One morning, Bill suddenly received a text message from Jennifer. Receiving a text from someone we don't normally correspond with that way invariably gets our attention, which it did for Bill. Like most of us, his first thought was, "I sure hope this is good news and not bad." Jennifer had an urgent issue she wanted to review with Bill, and she needed to meet that day, though she promised there was nothing wrong.

When they got together, Jennifer's urgent news turned out

to be that she'd been promoted to manager. She wanted to share the news in person with Bill. Her excitement was contagious, and she was off to celebrate with her friends. Bill and Jennifer agreed to get together in the coming weeks.

Shortly after, Bill hears again from Jennifer. She prefers not to meet over lunch or coffee but wants focused time with him. Now that she has her own office, Jennifer asks if they could meet there. Bill can tell she's proud of having a personal office, and he is excited to go there for their meeting. He's looking forward to expanding their discussion to new topics and challenges.

A few days later, Bill's in Jennifer's office. There's nothing on her desk except a computer and her office phone, but she's beaming with pride.

Bill begins, "Tell me about your new role and how it all happened."

Jennifer shares her story, "I had heard through the grapevine that Rob was getting a promotion, though nothing was official at the time. Then I got a phone call from Rob. He wanted me to come see him in his office. I thought to myself that he was going to tell me about what was going on for him and was pleased that I'd be one of the first to officially know.

"I walked in, sat down, and the first thing Rob said to me was the he had exciting news for both of us. I wondered what it could be and was now even more curious. Rob told me that he'd been promoted and was stepping out of his manager's role. He was moving up to the director level, which was something he'd been working on for a long time. While he was telling me about his new position, all I could think about was what the good news for me could be. I was only half listening to him and trying not to get too excited. I was hoping I'd get promoted, too.

"Then Rob told me that the leadership team had met, and they decided to do something they normally don't do. They were going to promote me because they thought it was natural for me to take Rob's place and step into the manager's role! Rob congratulated me and told me that I deserved it. He shared that I had done a great job demonstrating leadership qualities without actually being a leader and that I had earned the opportunity."

Bill congratulates Jennifer again and reinforces what a rarity it is that Flagler didn't post the opening. "Clearly, you must have done a great job of impressing Rob and his peers for them to feel so confident in you.

"Well done, Jennifer! Now your journey changes. You need to start thinking more seriously about being a leader, now that it's official. You've got this great office, and people will start looking at you and treating you differently. But remember, you have to be genuine. You have to be yourself!

"Are you ready to jump in? I have lots of ideas about leadership that I want to share with you. I think, for the next few months, we should get together at least monthly."

ASSESSING INDIVIDUALS

"The first thing I want to talk to you about is managing your direct reports."

"Of course," Jennifer agrees, "that's exactly what I'd like to know more about now that I've moved into Rob's role. I have seven people reporting to me, and I definitely need to learn how to manage them. I've watched Rob over the last few years, and there are a few things I would like to do differently."

Bill jumps in, "Exactly, you need to learn from Rob. He was a terrific leader for you, and it paid off by you being able to step into his role. Fortunately, you have the unique benefit of already knowing everyone on the team, but you can't take anything for granted. Just because you knew everyone as a peer, you have to get to know them in a new way now that you're a leader, which is not a bad thing. It's just different."

Jennifer asks, "I'm not sure I understand why you say I need to get acquainted with them again. I think I already know everyone on the team pretty well."

"You know them as your peers, which is true," Bill explains, "but for you to manage them as employees, you need to get to know them in a different way. You have to become acquainted with your team as their leader, not their friend. Some people on the team will be excited that you were promoted, others will be nice just because you're their leader, and still others may resent your good fortune. Remember, no one had a chance to interview for the job, and some people on the team may feel they're more qualified than you. You have to be prepared for resentment. You won't be able to help your team navigate their ongoing growth and satisfaction with work if you don't know what motivates them. This clearly is a situation you want to walk into with your eyes wide open.

"It's important that you spend quality one-on-one time with each team member in order to get to know them as individuals. Remember back when you were in the staff meeting and you didn't bring things up because you felt it wasn't your place to do so? You acted differently in a staff meeting than you did as an individual. You'll notice the same thing with the people on your team. They'll act differently in meetings than they do when you're having lunch with them. They'll demonstrate other traits when they relate to you as a leader instead of a peer.

"Don't forget that you are no longer one of the girls. You are the boss now. The team will view you differently and, in turn, you need to view them differently. Your goal still is to have great relationships; they will just be different relationships. You need to be conscious of the differences in your encounters with the team. Don't shy away from it. Be aware and embrace the change."

"Okay. I'm getting the difference," Jennifer says. "I want to give it a try."

Bill continues, "There are some basic things to consider when you're leading your team. Think about the rigor and style you want to maintain. It's up to you to decide what works best for you. You'll also want to find out what matters most for each team member, whether it's time off, compensation, the opportunity to learn, or career growth. Not everyone will have the same goals. What motivates you may be very different than what drives the people on your team.

> New roles mean new relationships. Don't resist the evolution of those relationships; it will lead to failure.

"You may have people on your team who are excited to come to work because they're learning something new. Another person may feel he knows how to do his job really well and is more concerned with being able to spend time with his family. The reason why you want to understand what motivates members of your team is not to be able to give them everything they want. It's so that you become aware of any landmines you may encounter as you go along. If there's someone on your team who values time off, they may resist working on weekends or staying late several nights in a row. On the other hand, if there's someone who is motivated by career growth, you could give her the opportunity to stay late and prove herself. You'll want to know who will be most excited by which opportunity. That's why understanding what's important to each individual is key to both their success and yours.

"The next thing to pay attention to is what's creating concern, anxiety, or even fear for your team members. I know fear sounds like a strong word to use in this context, Jennifer, but you want to develop your emotional intelligence so that you can find out what may be causing any negative reactions. For example, anyone who thought they should have had the same opportunity to move forward as you had may feel anxiety. If so, you'll want to address it directly and speak about it. You're going to have to figure these things out, both what motivates and what creates anxiety or fear.

"Lastly, you need to know what skills everyone has. What are their strengths and weaknesses? What makes them excel in their positions? That will probably be easier for you to determine because you've already worked on projects with everyone on the team and have seen them in action. Because your vantage point will be different now, you don't want to prejudge anyone, even though you will be able to take advantage of the knowledge you have from when you were peers to enlarge your understanding."

Bill goes on, "I suggest before you start assessing people's strengths and weaknesses, that you meet with Human Resources and have them explain to you how they do appraisals. In fact, they could be of help in fully understanding all the requirements involved with being a manager. I'm sure they have various tools you could take advantage of. You don't need to start everything from scratch. You'll want to gain access to as many resources as you can to help you become an outstanding leader.

> Beginning leaders should draw upon organizational practices. Renegade leadership is not usually welcomed from new leaders. Stay the organizational leadership course.

"Of course, when you're having conversations with your team members, be respectful of their boundaries and sensitive to their individuality. You don't want to ask them directly about their fears or anxiety. Be conversational. Building trust takes time.

"In the past, I've found that preparing a list of six or so questions can be helpful. I always ran the questions by HR to make sure I wasn't asking anything that would get me or the company in trouble. But what worked for me will probably be different than what works for you. Create your own list of the things you want to find out about each team member and use it as an opportunity for building trust and respect. If you're being careful, don't be afraid to ask the right questions. Trust your instincts. You earned this opportunity to be a manager because you were viewed as someone who could provide leadership. You wouldn't be in this position if Flagler didn't feel you couldn't handle it."

"I understand," Jennifer replies, "but I'd like you to walk me through an experience that you've had assessing your team's strengths and weaknesses. What did you learn that helped you do a better job providing leadership to your team?"

"I've got an interesting situation going on right now," Bill tells her. "Grace is a leader who reports to me and does a great job running her team. She's seen as one of the best interviewers we have on the team and one of the best mentors in the entire company; people regularly go to her for advice. Everyone wants Grace to interview their candidates. She's also known as a top-notch developer of people. However, I have a challenge with Grace.

"She doesn't excel in the administrative side of her role, and I'm being polite when I put it that way. Grace shies away from that part of the business. She's the queen of procrastination for anything dealing with expense reports, time sheets, and the like. She always waits until the very last minute. Eventually, I had to make a decision. Was I going to let my view of Grace's brand deteriorate because she's not strong administratively? Was I going to harbor a negative opinion of her in spite of her excellent leadership, mentorship, and metrics skills?

"I had to do some soul searching. Was I going to let Grace's lack of administrative skills interfere with my opinion of her? It took me nearly a year to reconcile the situation. I finally came to the conclusion that though administration is her weakness, she works hard and is focused on the right things. How did I want Grace to spend her time? In getting her administrative work done so that my life would be easier? Or did I prefer to have Grace focus on developing great talent and bringing good candidates to the team?

"It seems like an easy enough question when I put it like that, but I had to do my own checks and balances. I realized that because Grace is so strong in certain areas, I was willing to give in to her administrative shortcomings.

"Does that mean I let Grace off the hook on the administrative side? Absolutely not. The person I let off the hook was me. I don't stress over it anymore. I still put pressure on Grace to do a good job with her administrative tasks. But I'm not going to let it interfere with or diminish my relationship with her because she does so many other valuable things. Grace is one of our stars, and I had to reevaluate my expectations, not hers.

"Now, Jennifer, some people may disagree and think what I'm doing is not right, that people should be graded on their entire performance. The way I see it is we speak about people's strengths and weaknesses because there are *always* going to be weaknesses. As a leader, I believe it's my job to know what areas I want people to be strong in and be willing to give in a little on their weaknesses. If Grace had been strong in administrative skill but weak in her metrics and mentoring, maybe I would have felt differently and not want her on the team.

"Where do you think she brings more value to Flagler? It's obvious, right?

"How was I able to come to this conclusion and why do I share it with you, Jennifer? It's because Grace and I put time and energy into our relationship. We understand each other, and working with Grace on the areas she needs to improve helped me better my coaching skills. I want to stress, Jennifer, if someone has weakness, don't give in. Hold the person accountable, but don't end up stressing over it yourself."

> Put leadership energy into improving strengths, followed by managing weaknesses.

THE VALUE OF ONE-ON-ONE MEETINGS

Jennifer tells Bill, "This is all so helpful. I'm really grateful that we set up extra time today to talk. How do you recommend I start getting reacquainted with my team members? As you said, I already know all seven of them."

Bill immediately offers, "Jennifer, we spoke about one-on-one meetings. To me a one-on-one meeting is something you put on the calendar for an entire year. You schedule a meeting every week or every other week continuously. The meetings should last thirty minutes to an hour. I recommend that for the first month, you do them weekly for no more than a half hour.

"You want to take your time to learn about each person.

As the leader, you set the time frame of your meetings. Initially setting up shorter time frames will minimize anxiety when preparing for the meeting.

After that, you can reevaluate and maybe go to forty-five-minute sessions every other week, depending on what makes the most sense for you and your team members. Whatever you decide, make sure you are consistent. Don't have a one-on-one meeting for an hour with one person and thirty minutes with another. They'll see it as you playing favorites. And who's to say which one would be the favorite, the person you meet with for an hour or the one that gets thirty minutes!"

Jennifer chuckles, "You're right. I don't know which would be better, more or less time with the boss."

"Exactly. You never know what the perception will be, so always be consistent. The important thing is that when you're meeting with each team member, you take the time to understand what their goals are.

Consistency helps manage the perception of favoritism.

"A great way to start the first meeting is to go over a previous performance review. I realize you don't have any experience giving performance reviews, but you certainly have received them. You could begin by asking each team member what they think of the way Rob reviewed them. It would be a nonthreatening way for you to find out how they've been doing, and it could serve as an opportunity to create a level of vulnerability between you and your employees based on what another person—Rob in this case—said. If there's anything they don't agree with, they can share it with you. As I mentioned earlier, you don't want to ask explicit questions about their fears or concerns. This could be an opening for them to speak candidly.

"The other important thing I want to make sure you do is to take notes when you're having your one-on-one meetings, whether in a notebook, on your computer, or any other way that works for you. Then stay on top of it, which, of course, you already know is essential, being a project manager. You appreciate better than most people how important it is to follow up. One of the quickest way to lose respect with your team members is by not following through."

Bill summarizes, "With regard to one-on-one meetings, more is better than less. When I was in college, I preferred classes with multiples tests and lots of pop quizzes over those in which the entire grade depended on the final exam. When I had lots of tests, I always knew how I was doing. I think the same thing holds true for employees. When they have lots of evaluations, it creates a base of understanding and fairness in your relationships with them.

"I have one more thing to add. At some point when you're consulting with HR—and this doesn't have to happen right away—you might want to check with them about their expectations for performance reviews. How did Rob do performance reviews?"

"Rob only did performance reviews once a year," Jennifer answers. "He'd write up his thoughts on a piece of a paper, and that was it."

"Do you think that was effective?" Bill asks Jennifer.

"It was great when it happened," she says, "but then it would be a long time before there was another one."

"In my department," Bill explains, "we're expected to conduct performance reviews with our team members four times a year. We do one major performance review annually, and then we meet three additional times with each employee to check in and see how they're performing relative to the goals we laid out. It's different than how things were done in your area. To be honest, I'm not sure I know whether or not there are company guidelines for performance reviews, which is why I think it's a good idea for you to check in with HR and find out from them."

Jennifer declares, "I like your way a lot better."

"I understand, Jennifer, but my way may not be the right way. You're a new leader, and I'd like to see you do things the way Flagler wants them done, not the way Rob or I do them."

"Good point," Jennifer says.

Bill adds, "For all I know, there may be some specific HR trainings to help you.

"I also want to bring up again something we reviewed earlier. You're in a unique situation because you were once a peer with everyone on your team, which could be a good thing. From what you've been saying, it sounds like most of the team think your promotion is positive. Is there anyone whom you think is not excited about it?"

"Yes." Jennifer admits. "There is a guy named Gary, and we used to work well together, but now it feels like he's giving me the cold shoulder. I think maybe he feels he should have been given an opportunity to advance."

"Okay," Bill comments. "In one of your first few meetings with Gary, gently try to raise the topic. Ask Gary what he wants out of his career. If he says he wants to grow, that'll be a clue. See if you can work through the issue with him. Try to alleviate any resentment he may have toward you. Though Gary may not be happy, his resentment shouldn't be directed at you, Jennifer. You could use the situation as an opportunity to help Gary grow professionally, but first you'll have to sort through his concerns.

"Remember that Gary probably has anxiety over the change, which could create angst when having a conversation. My recommendation is to schedule Gary first to get the discussion over with. Then start to manage any concerns Gary has or stress you have related to the conversation and move forward. Go into the conversation caring about Gary's concerns, but remain confident in your approach. Use the situation as an opportunity to build trust with Gary.

> Trust as a leader is earned and looks different than trust as a peer. Earn it early.

"The bottom line is you want to make everyone feel at ease during your transition. Be transparent and direct with your team. Put all the issues on the table. The more up front you are about any concerns regarding you being a new leader or anything else, the more you'll create engagement and trust within the team.

"On a slightly different note," Bill remarks, "find out how team members prefer to communicate. If you need to contact anyone urgently, what's the best way to do it? Do they want to be texted? Do they want you to call them on their cell? Should you send an instant message?

"With my team, I noticed that people often had their instant messaging turned off so they wouldn't get distracted while they were working. I used to assume they were offline and weren't doing anything, so we agreed that if I needed to reach anyone urgently, I would send a text. That's what works for us. For regular matters, we use email or instant message. We worked through the issue collectively. Never let technology be the barrier for team growth. Perhaps someone's computer breaks down and they don't tell you. You never want to jump to any false conclusions."

WORK-BASED RELATIONSHIPS

"Before you leave, Bill, do you have any more personal stories you could share with me?"

Bill offers, "I have one that dates from the job I had before I came to Flagler.

"My previous company was located outside the city in a

fairly remote area, so I used to have lunch with people on my leadership team fairly regularly. There were only two or three places nearby to eat, and one was the company cafeteria.

"We'd talk about work over lunch, or our families. We'd talk about all kinds of things going on in our lives. I didn't realize it at the time, but I was making a mistake. I was building personal relationships with my employees, and it was making it difficult for me to be objective when it came to work. Even more importantly, I wasn't being fair to the people I didn't have lunch with.

"My mistake was not the lunch or the time together. It was letting those friendships bleed into my decision-making process. I was not treating everyone equally. I was letting personal relationships impact my leadership.

"As I matured as a leader, I had to learn that work friendships are great, but they should *never* impact decision making. Here at Flagler, I'll occasionally go to lunch with one of my direct reports, but it's rare. I don't want to give the impression that I'm favoring one person over another, and I don't want to get myself into a situation where I'm compromising my leadership. As we discussed earlier, consistency is a key attribute of leadership.

"As you know, Jennifer, I travel a lot for Flagler, frequently with one of my team members. It's natural in those circumstances to go out to dinner together or sit next to each other on the plane. It's easy to build relationships in those situations, and I don't resist it. I've developed friendships with a number of people I work with, but I try hard not to let the friendship influence my ability to manage them. We spoke about Dan earlier, Kelsey's old boss. Dan and I travel together all the time and have built a good relationship. Of course, we're going to have dinner together.

"The difference is now I don't seek it out. It's simply a natural consequence of work whereas before I used to seek out the opportunity to dine with people I was leading. There have been several instances when I've had to give Dan direct and honest feedback that he hasn't always wanted to hear. But Dan has told me that he admires the fact that we can be friends in certain settings and that I'll never compromise our professional relationship because of it.

"Now, I believe that being able to have dinner with someone like Dan and not be the boss at dinner has helped me become a better leader. It made our relationship stronger."

Jennifer jumps in, "But that seems to contradict what you just said. Why are you saying this?"

"Becoming friends enabled us to have greater trust and respect for each other professionally because we've gotten to know each other as people. The key to all of this is to be consistent. Just because I developed a relationship with Dan, I don't treat him differently. But I do understand him better than others and recognize why he responds in certain situations, which allows me to give him better insight and coaching because I know what makes him tick.

"No one wants to be viewed as someone's favorite. As you start your journey as a manager, be sure you treat everyone equally. Of course, you'll need to spend more time with some people if they need help or if they're excelling, but never appear to play favorites."

"Thanks so much, Bill. You've given me a lot to think about today. What do you want me to work on until we meet again?"

"I know I talked about a lot today, Jennifer. Give yourself time to take it all in. In the short term, focus on the one-on-one meetings. There's plenty more to discuss, but for now, let's deal with the one-on-ones. Document the conversations, including goals and strengths, that you have with each person. And because Gary might be resentful, be sure to put energy into that relationship. See it as a leadership challenge and an opportunity to work on a relationship that's not starting off on the right foot."

A FEW MONTHS LATER

As it's been a while since Bill and Jennifer have seen each other, Bill decides to stop by Jennifer's office one day when he happens to be in her building. When he shows up, she's working, and he asks if he can borrow a few minutes of her time. He wants to hear how things have been going.

Jennifer seems pleased to see him, which Bill interprets as a good sign.

The first thing Jennifer mentions is that her instincts about Gary were right. He definitely was resentful of the opportunity Jennifer received, but she feels they're heading in the right direction. She's trying to cultivate a relationship of allies with Gary. He seems to be letting his guard down and is beginning to work more closely with her. She's going to continue focusing on him.

Jennifer also feels good about how her one-on-one meetings are going and is eager to learn the next steps in the process.

Bill reminds Jennifer, "Stick to your commitment regarding one-on-one meetings. Don't stress if you miss one because you're traveling; just make sure you communicate with your team members.

"When you do your one-on-one meetings:

- Be open and receptive to feedback from your team members; a one-on-one meeting works in both directions: for you to give them feedback and vice versa.
- Create an environment that encourages honest dialogue; to be successful, a one-on-one meeting requires an investment from both sides; the worst is when only one person does all the talking.
- Always follow up on the outcomes.

"Other than that, it sounds like you're on the right track, Jennifer. I look forward to our next meeting."

Chapter 6

✳

Lead the Way: Guiding Your Team

It's been a while since Bill has heard from Jennifer, and he's starting to get concerned. He's learned from the past that not hearing from her may not be a good sign, so he decides to do things differently. He feels it's time to take the initiative. Bill phones Jennifer to check in and see how's she's doing.

During their conversation, Jennifer reveals that she's been feeling overwhelmed. Though she's been having one-on-one meetings with her team members, she hasn't held a staff meeting yet and is nervous about jumping in.

Bill responds encouragingly, saying that it's appropriate for her to feel overwhelmed. Even though she came highly prepared to the job, it's still a new role, and she has responsibility for seven individuals. Whenever we do anything new, even if it's simply eating a new type of food, things are different. Bill encourages Jennifer not to get overly concerned. It's only natural that she feels the way she does. He also suggests that she go ahead and schedule her first staff meeting, and then they can get together in a couple weeks to talk about how it went.

A few weeks pass, and this time Jennifer goes to Bill's office instead of meeting in her office or over lunch. They need to have a more serious discussion. Whenever there's something more difficult to work through, Bill prefers to meet a mentee in one of their offices. This approach minimizes distractions and sets a tone that the meeting is going to be focused.

Bill begins the conversation by asking how things are going in general. "Are you still feeling overwhelmed?"

Jennifer shares that she had her first staff meeting. "It was good to get it out of the way."

Bill asks, "Was that the first time you met with everyone altogether?"

"No," Jennifer explains. "I took everyone out for a team-building lunch, and that went really well. We socialized, got to know each other better, and talked about all the changes that have happened. I think it was good to do, though we made it more of a kickoff celebration as a new team.

"After that, we had our first staff meeting, and to be honest, I felt like I was back in Rob's staff meeting again, except I was Rob! And I didn't like it at all. I felt like I was just a fill-in for Rob."

Bill wants to know more. "What didn't you like? Are you saying you don't like the way Rob ran meetings?"

> Professional development includes observing leadership traits we don't like and pushing against those leadership muscles.

"In fact, I don't," Jennifer answers. "I always felt he created an environment that wasn't conducive for having a good discussion. Rob had a way in which he would stymie the dialogue."

"What do you mean by stymie the dialogue? That's an interesting choice of words," Bill says.

Having thought about it a lot, Jennifer is quick to respond. "Remember when we first met and I told you about going to staff meetings and not talking? Partly it was my fault, but it was also due to the fact that Rob didn't encourage participation from everyone in the meetings. He clearly had his favorites. If he didn't like what someone was saying, you could see it in his body language. He'd cross his arms, lean back, and give the impression that he really wasn't interested in what the person was saying. Often, he'd just end the discussion and say it was time to move on to another topic.

"All of us on the team were tuned in to whether Rob liked what we were saying or not. If he didn't, we just dropped it and gave up."

"You gave up?" Bill interjects. "That's another strong choice of words."

"Yeah," Jennifer replies, "we gave up on the dialogue."

Bill says, "Well, we've all witnessed that, haven't we? We've all had bosses like that. It sounds like Rob might have been the type of leader who gets impatient. But he also had good traits. He believed in you and encouraged you in your one-on-one meetings. You've mentioned a lot of positive things about Rob in the past."

"You're right. I did. I just didn't like going to his staff meetings because it always felt like it was his agenda, not ours."

Bill pauses a moment. "I want you to think carefully about what you just articulated. You said it was Rob's agenda, not the team's agenda. How did you feel about that?"

"I didn't like it. It wasn't a team meeting. It was Rob's meeting."

"Okay," Bill carries on, "you said that you didn't like it as a team member, and you also just told me that when you had your first staff meeting, you ran it in the same way Rob did. I think you've identified something you're probably going to want to change—how can you make your staff meeting feel like a team meeting? In fact, let's call them team meetings instead of staff meetings. How can you guide your team in a direction that you'd like them to take without running the meeting according to your agenda only?"

"I like that way of thinking," Jennifer replies. "Maybe that's why I felt so awkward sitting in Rob's seat! I must have felt like I should be acting like Rob since I was now the one running the meeting. But your point is a good one. I should be acting like me, not Rob!"

Bill jumps in, "We could almost end our conversation here, Jennifer, because if there's one thing you need to do, it's create your own style of running a meeting. Remember when we spoke about having your own culture and brand? Well, it includes how you deal with your team as well. I don't want us to get too focused on the staff meeting issue but to consider, instead, how to create opportunities for bringing the team together."

"Bill, you keep referring to 'leading the team.' I'm working with a group of project managers, and we all operate as independents when we work on projects. We don't function as a team the way others do. What makes you say a team environment is important for us?"

Bill explains, "The team concept is important in all work contexts for a number of reasons. Many professionals work individually: in hospitals and in health care in general, for example, or in delivery services or wherever individuals carry out their jobs on their own. But even so, whenever a group of people report to a single leader, like your team does with you, it creates an atmosphere of unity. People start to feel comfortable reaching out to one another. They have someone they can go to and ask for help when they need cover during their paid time off, for example. There's the potential for peer-to-peer support. Clearly, that results in a productivity gain for you as a leader and for the team as individuals. It's a win for everyone.

"Belonging to a team also tends to minimize a sense of competition. Of course, healthy competition is good in the work environment, but at the same time, you don't want competitiveness to get out of control. You want to establish a sense of synergy so that employees feel like they're in it together.

> Team meetings are an excellent training ground for growing as a leader—a small environment, lots of dynamics, and chances for leadership at-bats.

"Barriers come down among individuals who are on teams, and everyone improves. When employees have a sense of community, which is the key word to focus on, they work better, are more productive, and share best practices. They can draw on each other's experiences and not feel isolated or alone. That's why it's important that your goal is to create a team and not a group of individual performers."

"I love the idea of creating a community and synergies within the team! But where do I begin? We talked about team meetings; is that where I should start?" Jennifer asks.

"You said it best yourself," Bill replies. "Common wisdom says that any time a person steps into a new leadership role, they should find the one thing the previous leader did best and harness that strength. But I think it's more interesting and fun to identify the thing they didn't do well and change that. It provides an opportunity to start bringing one's own culture and personality to the team.

"When you mentioned staff meetings, Jennifer, it reminded me that when I was starting out in my career I used to be weak in creating a nurturing environment. I was a lot like Rob. I had strong opinions and got a lot of negative feedback. 'Impatient' was the word that was used a lot. I didn't cultivate an environment of innovation or dialogue. I was focused on my agenda only, which sounds similar to Rob.

"In staff meetings, I always pushed my ideas and didn't stimulate team dialogue. I would wait a short period for discussion, and then I became impatient and ended the dialogue. As I matured, I started to lean in to the conversations, encourage dialogue, and not end the discussion with my opinions. I learned to grow my team members by giving them the freedom to share their ideas in a safe and healthy environment. The entire team, including me, was better for it.

"I challenged myself to improve and worked hard on creating a team culture of free speech. I wanted to encourage people to share their opinions, whether it was during a one-on-one meeting with me or in a staff meeting.

"Of course, we always maintained an atmosphere of decorum and respect appropriate to a work environment, but at the same time, I encouraged sharing ideas. It wasn't always easy, especially when I had more experience than the person just starting out. I'd think what they were saying was impractical and wanted to move on, but I was the one being immature. I had to restrain myself from expressing my opinion and made an effort to allow team members to share theirs. I knew that was the way they would grow and develop self-confidence.

"An unexpected outcome of having open dialogues was the creation of healthy tension during the discussion. With a safety net for sharing ideas in place, we had great conversations on topics that sparked conflicting ideas. Productive debates became intentional and led to better results.

"Now, did that mean everybody could say whatever they wanted and everyone's opinion was correct? No, of course not. At the end of the day, I was the leader. I was the one who made the decisions. As we already talked about, a good leader makes decisions. But I also believe in creating an environment that supports everyone being able to express their thoughts. I encourage you, since you didn't like the way Rob did things, to find your own way.

"I have to confess that when I started letting everyone

on the team share their opinions, great ideas came out. It was one plus one equals three. When I held them back, it was more like one plus seven equals one!"

TACTICAL AND STRATEGIC MEETINGS

"So, yes, continue with team meetings, Jennifer. As they are now, how would you describe them? What's one word that comes to mind if you had to classify the type of meetings they are?"

Jennifer thinks a moment. Her first thought is that they are boring and nonproductive, but the one word that comes to her mind is "tactical"—typically a good amount of time is spent in meetings talking about upcoming projects, and she shares her thoughts with Bill.

"Yes," Bill says, "that's generally how most people think of staff meetings, as a tactical event, which is why it's helpful to schedule them in a predictable, ongoing sequence.

"I also like to schedule regular strategic meetings with my team. Because they provide an opportunity to focus on the future, I call them quarterly business reviews, or QBRs, even though I may not always hold them on a quarterly basis. Sometimes I do them less frequently. The point is that I get my team together, and we spend 100 percent of our time focusing on six to eighteen months into the future, and when we feel the timing is right, we may even look further out. We also keep an eye on the three-year business plan, but our main goal is to explore how we can improve in the coming months.

"I encourage you to have strategic meetings, too, Jennifer. Figure out a rhythm that works for the team. Perhaps you'll want to bring your team together every three months. It doesn't have to be a big production. You could easily meet in the cafeteria, bring in some coffee, and keep it simple. The purpose is to meet regularly to discuss the future. How can you improve? How is productivity? You may want to consider other long-term issues, like annual planning.

"The real value of having regular strategic business reviews is to give your team an opportunity to think innovatively and strategically. Most of our time at work is focused on the short term and daily activities. We don't think about the future much, but I believe it can make a big difference in your team members' professional experience."

"That sounds exciting! I've never been to a meeting like that," Jennifer exclaims.

Strategic meetings allow a team to grow spatially, which leads to improved performance. A strategic mindset can produce great insights that benefit customers and partners.

Bill tells Jennifer that his next quarterly business review is coming up in a few weeks. "We're meeting in the conference room of the finance department. It's a three-hour meeting, and you are more than welcome to sit in as an observer. It will give you a sense of what a strategic meeting is like. But remember, we're finance people. Some issues may be irrelevant for you, but many of the ideas and the concepts should be similar to your area.

"What I love about doing these strategic meetings is that they allow me to lead the team in a different way than I do on a day-to-day basis. I think you'd enjoy the change as well. It stretches your mind and I promise it will make you a better leader. Your team won't be surprised when the future becomes the present."

It's time for Bill and Jennifer to wrap up, and Bill wants to make sure he shares a few key points that are critical because Jennifer has been stressing over her new leadership responsibilities. He summarizes the next steps.

"So, Jennifer, make sure you come to our departmental strategic meeting. I'll send you a calendar invite. Also:

- Write down—don't just think about it—what you liked most about Rob's leadership style and the traits you want to embrace, along with the one thing you disliked the most.

- Consider how you're going to change the atmosphere in team meetings from the perspective of the team, not according to what it will mean for you. Be intentional and put your brand into your leadership.
- Lastly, schedule meetings, your one-on-ones, staff meetings, and strategic reviews. You can always change them if needed. Regularity will give your team a sense of security; they've just gone through a big change, too, and may have some anxiety about the future.

"You're doing a great job, Jennifer. Continue to focus on running meetings better. There are plenty of helpful books and articles on the topic. Find out what works best for you. Don't hesitate to express your brand and culture with the team. They will feed off your strength and grow professionally. Encourage feedback on how you can do things better as a group. Remember, they're coming from an environment where feedback was not encouraged. Cultivating transparency will be an easy win for you as a leader."

Chapter 7

———— ✳ ————

Build Structure: Organizing Your Team

Since Jennifer attended Bill's strategic meeting, they've been getting together informally over coffee. Bill sees these casual, one-on-one meetings as an opportunity to provide encouragement and support to Jennifer as she settles into her new role as a leader. He doesn't want to overwhelm her at this point in their mentoring process. He's there for Jennifer if she has questions or concerns, but because she's going through a lot of change becoming a leader and getting to know her team in new ways, he doesn't want to add anything more to the mix. Mainly, they chat about personal things—what's going outside of work, how Jennifer is handling stress, and her experiences with the project management association.

In every mentor-mentee relationship, there will be moments when major career-defining events take place. For much of the time, however, the focus will be on reinforcing insights from previous conversations, providing an outlet for the mentee to speak candidly about whatever may be going on in his or her professional or personal life, and supporting the routine challenges one encounters in any job.

> Mentors should not feel pressured to constantly introduce new tips and tricks. Many times, their role is to listen and reassure. Being a sounding board is a key function of a mentor.

A major role of a football coach is to drill the team on plays and tactics they already know. A coach doesn't introduce new plays or concepts at every practice. Similarly, rather than give Jennifer new tips each time they meet, Bill's job is to assist her in becoming more proficient in the skills she already has and to help alleviate any anxiety she might be experiencing. For the past three to four months, Bill refrained from suggesting anything new.

FACING CHALLENGES

Four months quickly pass, and soon Jennifer reaches out to Bill, telling him that she's eager to have a session with him.

When they meet, Jennifer jumps right in. "I have a problem. I think I know how to handle it, but I need your advice."

"Okay," Bill responds, "what's the problem? Walk me through it."

"As you know," Jennifer launches in, "Flagler is in the middle of becoming a publicly traded company. Because we're in the process of making the transition, there's a big focus on finances right now."

"Yes," Bill acknowledges, "I'm definitely aware of that. It's what I've been spending most of my time on lately."

Jennifer continues, "We've just been handed a wave of new projects, which amounts to nearly a 15 percent increase in our workload. Like we've always done in the past, I asked leadership for additional staff to handle it, but because of cost concerns, they refused. So that means I need to improve the team's productivity by 15 percent without taking a step backwards in our process and procedures or reducing the quality of our work!"

"How do you feel about that?" Bill asks.

"I'm stressed about it! And I'm not eating right and feel like my team sees my anxiety. This is one of my first real challenges. I don't want my boss to lose faith in me, and I don't want to let my team down," Jennifer admits. "I've never been in a situation like this before. When I was a project manager and had a special project, I simply worked harder to get it done. But that was me. I was willing to put in the overtime. The situation feels different now. I have seven team members whom I want to be productive. Sometimes to increase productivity, quality has to be sacrificed, but I've been told that can't happen. I can't compromise quality, and I can't get additional staff, so I have to improve productivity. I feel I have a unique challenge ahead of me."

Bill thinks for a minute and then says, "Your situation is not all that unique. These kinds of things go on every day in the world of work. They just don't happen all that often here at Flagler. It will be a great learning experience for you to guide your team through a process of increasing productivity without losing quality. Just think of it as another leadership at-bat and a chance to tackle new challenges.

"Let me ask you one question before we get into this. How would you rate the morale of your team?"

"On a scale of one to ten, I'd give it an eight, with ten being the best."

"Excellent. It sounds like you have good team morale. It also sounds as if this push for increased productivity could be a permanent thing. Do you think that's true?" Bill pursues.

"You're right. I don't think it's a temporary, three-month situation," Jennifer answers. "I'm taking the approach that it's an ongoing demand."

"So, we can assume for now that there'll be ongoing growth, without new staff," Bill points out. "If that's the case, what would you like your team's morale to be in three months' time? Do you want it to remain at eight?"

Having never thought about it, Jennifer replies, "Well, yes. I'd want it to stay around seven or eight. I don't want to lose team members over this. I feel my team is highly engaged right now and I don't want that to change."

"Great. You just laid out the parameters we have to work within," Bill explains. "You have to increase productivity by 15 percent, you can't add staff, you don't want team morale to be negatively impacted, and you want the high level of employee engagement to stay as it is. And is it fair to say that you also don't want any employee turnover?"

"Yes, that's right. I would add that as a parameter," Jennifer says.

Bill goes on, "It's true that you're facing a significant business challenge, but at the same time, you have a wonderful opportunity to provide leadership to your team. And I'll go one step further. I think you have a great opportunity to provide leadership to Flagler as well. You could help the company preserve its financially conservative position while it sustains growth. I think the situation has excitement written all over it, but it will be challenging.

"Let's think it through. How can you accomplish all of that?" Bill questions.

"The easiest way to begin solving this problem—and one that every leader will resort to at first—is to determine whether everyone on the team is as productive as they should be. What's the case with your team, Jennifer? Is everybody as productive as you would like them to be? Do you have the right people? Let's walk through that assessment."

Jennifer and Bill discuss each of the seven team members and evaluate their performance. As they go through the exercise, Bill is careful that Jennifer doesn't expect everyone to be exceeding expectations. The goal is to determine only whether anyone is not meeting expectations. Employee evaluations focus on satisfying or exceeding expectations, while in this case, Bill only wants Jennifer to identify anyone who is working below expectations.

At the end of the review, Jennifer singles out a couple of individuals who are functioning slightly below normal, so Bill gives her a homework assignment.

"I'd like you to think about why the two people you identified are not meeting expectations. Is it because of the role they're in? Is it due to a lack of training? Does it have to do with their personality? Is there anything you might be missing? For example, could something be occurring in their personal life that is affecting their work?

"One way I like to think about managing a team is like making a sculpture," Bill shares. "Though I never was an artist in school, I think of the team as my clay, and I'm the sculptor. You could just as easily use the analogy of a painter—the team are the colors you have to work with to create a beautiful painting. It's our job as leaders to turn individuals, who are the equivalent of the artist's clay or tubes of paint, into a work of art—into a well-functioning, productive team."

Jennifer considers what she heard, "I think I get what you're pointing to, though I didn't choose the seven people on my team—or, in other words, the clay I have to work with."

In most instances, the opportunity to build a team from scratch doesn't exist. The ability to adapt and understand your team is critical to success.

"That's right. You didn't hire any of those people. They were given to you as your team. Your job is to transform them into a highly productive group of individuals. That's your mission."

"I like it!" Jennifer exclaims.

MICRO- AND MACROLEADERSHIP

"We've all heard a colleague complain that their boss is micromanaging them," Bill continues, "and we think it's a bad thing. I disagree. I want to share with you what I call microleadership.

"We hear the word micromanagement all the time. No one likes to be micromanaged, but it's rare to hear someone speak about microleadership."

Jennifer questions, "What is microleadership? I've heard of micromanagement, but not microleadership."

Bill grabs his phone and searches for the definition of micromanage and shares it with Jennifer. "Micromanagement is defined as 'management with excessive control or attention to details.' To me, microleadership is providing leadership by understanding the fine details of a situation.

In order to obtain that kind of detail, you need to make an effort to understand roles and circumstances. The goal of microleadership is to lead, not to control.

"Micromanagement describes the leader who goes into all the details. The negative connotation is that the boss doesn't let you work on your own or take initiative. She's always looking into your affairs. To be honest, since you're a new leader, I think you should consider adopting microleadership and becoming more involved with your teams' business. You need to understand what they're doing if you want to be able to direct them. How can you lead if you don't know what they're doing?

"A positive interpretation of microleadership, I believe, refers to someone who takes the time to get to know people—a leader who gives the gift of her time to team members in order to better understand what they're doing. The goal is to help everyone become better at what they do.

"Of course, there are plenty of bad examples of micromanagement, but we don't need to talk about that. I want to focus on the idea of consciously microleading for the purpose of becoming acquainted with the day-to-day activities of each member of your

> Microleadership is valuable for short periods of time. Long-term microleadership indicates that there's a problem, either with the leader or a team member.

team. The goal is to assist people in performing their jobs better. It's is a short-term, well-thought-through decision to lead in this manner.

"The purpose of macroleadership, on the other hand, is to express trust in people's abilities and allow them to do their jobs. In macroleadership, the leader is more hands-off and watching from afar to give team members the opportunity to grow, take risks, and make mistakes. When you're developing a team, you want to adopt a macromanagement style to encourage taking on bigger challenges. You want to grow and nurture skills and responsibilities of team members and create trust by providing enough space for people to do their work. But remember, taking risks and making mistakes go together."

Jennifer comments, "I thought we were focusing on helping my team become more productive. I'm not sure why you're telling me about micro- and macroleadership."

Bill answers, "You're right. We are trying to figure out a way for your team to be more productive. However, if you don't fully understand what your team members are doing, you won't be able to coach them successfully. That's the microleadership component. The macroleadership part involves empowering them to be more productive. The two work together. Unless you know the strengths and weaknesses of each person through the microexperience, you won't be able to steer them in the right direction toward greater productivity.

"For example, if you have a team member that you know has poor project management skills, you wouldn't want to empower him to take on the largest project available. Perhaps you observed that person during interviews and realized that he's the best interviewer on the team. You could give him more opportunities to conduct interviews and less project management work. But you're not going to know these things without seeing people in action. And you're also not going to know how well he's growing professionally unless he's had a chance to take risks."

As their time together is winding down, Jennifer asks Bill if he has any more suggestions for her of things to do or any words of encouragement prior to their next meeting.

"I suggest you go back to your team and let them know about the challenge you've been given, that you need to increase productivity but can't bring in additional staff."

"Why would I share that with the team?" she asks Bill. "I think it will create stress."

"That's a risk I think is worth taking," Bill answers. "I

shared it's what I would do. I'd also share with them that over the coming month, you, as their leader, are going to work on finding ways to help them to increase productivity, and that you want to keep morale and engagement high at the same time. I think you should level with them that things are going to change. In addition—this is where I'd turn the situation into an opportunity—I'd ask for their advice.

"The reason to ask for their advice is to reinforce that they're part of the decision-making process. You're being transparent with the team. Fifteen percent growth means the company's not going out of business. In fact, it's giving you and the team a great opportunity to help Flagler in a successful journey. I recommend you present the situation as positive—as a welcomed opportunity to increase productivity.

"In any event, your team will feel the difference, so why not share the situation with them up front? They may come up with some great ideas if you ask for their input. Look at it as a development opportunity for your team!

"The last thing I want to say is that by openly sharing the situation with the team, you're building trust."

"Okay, but I still find the situation stressful," Jennifer confides.

"In any challenging work situation, there will always be some degree of healthy tension," Bill asserts.

"Healthy tension? I've never thought of tension as being healthy!"

"The situation you're in now is an example of healthy tension," Bill proposes. "The business is clearly growing, which is giving you the chance to contribute to that growth and success, which is a great thing. It's healthy for you and the company. You benefit when you develop in a positive environment. Through your macroleadership and bringing the team into the process of finding ways to be more productive, they'll also have the opportunity to experience healthy stress.

"Of course, there can be unhealthy tension at work too, but I'm asking you to find the right amount of tension that is constructive. That's why I recommend sharing the situation with the team and letting them be part of the process.

"Your homework assignment, not to forget, is to evaluate the two team members who are underperforming. Also, be sure to keep an eye on your micro- and macroleadership.

"Jennifer, I want to remind you that you're dealing with people's professional lives. You don't want to make any hasty decisions. Take the time to think things through and spend some time with the two individuals. Then we'll talk about them again so that we both are confident you're making good decisions. Lastly, share the situation with your team and create some healthy tension. Even if you bring them into the process, the decisions will ultimately be yours to make."

A MONTH GOES BY

Bill and Jennifer agree to meet in Jennifer's office. Bill's looking forward to hearing how she's been dealing with the leadership challenges she's facing. The first thing he wants to know is how things went when she shared the need for greater productivity with her team. Jennifer reports that they didn't come up with any silver bullets—no good ideas that were realistic—but she feels it was useful for them to have had the conversation. They won't have any surprises, and now they regularly take interest in how things are coming along, which is encouraging. All in all, it created more positive team engagement in ways she didn't anticipate.

"That's to be expected," Bill says. "Occasionally, some-one may come up with a great idea, but usually when you challenge a team, it's unlikely anything creative will emerge. Your team's job is to run projects, not figure out how to be more productive.

"And how did it go with the two individuals that you felt were not meeting expectations? What did you come up with? Where did the evaluation take you?"

"It was great," Jennifer answers. "Your advice was right. If I had given you an answer a month ago, it wouldn't have been the same one as now. A month ago, I would have said that they simply weren't productive and left it at that. Neither seemed to bring the same level of effort to their work as everyone else. After I spent time with them, however, I realized the problem wasn't a lack of effort, but efficiency.

"In fact, one of the two probably works harder than anyone on the team. He's just not efficient in how he does things. I doubt if a manager ever spent time helping him, so I'm excited about the opportunity to provide assistance. I've already noticed a few basics he could use help with, like how he interviews people and takes notes. I think he'll be a lot happier at work once he learns to be more efficient because he certainly puts in a lot of effort."

Bill understands. "Inefficiency is not something you want

on a daily basis! It sounds like this person is open-minded and could be receptive to coaching from you—a great opportunity for you to help someone go from not meeting expectations to meeting them. What about the other person?"

"The other person, to be honest, may not be in the right role," Jennifer admits.

Bill pauses. He's a little surprised to hear that. It's a serious conclusion for Jennifer to make. "So, tell me more," he asks. "Why do you think this person's not in the right role?"

"Our project managers are a small team," Jennifer explains, "so we have to be good at many things, but there are fundamentals that are essential—interviewing, for one. You also have to be good at taking notes, following up, and putting project plans together. There are other things, of course, but those four are nonnegotiables here at Flagler.

"What I've also observed is that this person has great interactive skills. She's probably best at interviewing as well as taking notes and creating a congenial work environment with the people she works with. But she doesn't do a great job following up on action items or preparing project plans, which in project management are vital. In fact, I think she's weak in those areas."

Bill digs deeper. "Are these areas you could help her to improve? Let's take following up because I don't fully understand what's involved with project planning, though I do know what it takes to follow up. Do you think you can teach her some of those skills?"

"Unfortunately, no. Having spent time with her, I've come to realize that she's not built that way."

"Great choice of words, Jennifer." Bill adds, "We're not all built to do the same job. You may not be built to work in the finance department, and I may not be built to work in project management. As we discussed before, I was not built for computer programming. It's an important consideration.

"You also stated that this person is best at interviewing and creating a great work environment with her internal customers. Those sound like they could be priceless skills in project management."

"That's true," Jennifer concurs. "One of my bigger challenges is that several of my team members don't have great interpersonal skills."

"What I suggest," Bill recommends, "in a situation like this, is to be careful not to let someone go. It's a last resort here at Flagler and the reason we enjoy such a great work environment. Our employee retention is excellent.

"Because this person does have some valuable skills, your homework is to figure out how you could alter her role to help her be more successful. Work on that and see if you can get her other skills to a level good enough for her to stay in her current role. You want to play to your team members' strengths, while also being aware of their weaknesses.

"This will require microleadership as you know, but at the macro level, perhaps this person could be given greater responsibility on the interactive side of the services you provide. Maybe you could find a way to reduce the time she spends doing follow-up and project planning. Give that a go, and view it as a timely, positive challenge for both you and your team member."

"Okay," Jennifer replies. "I like the challenge, and I also like the team member we're talking about. She's a wonderful person. I just need to get more out of her."

"One last thing," Bill carries on. "You haven't told me how you're going to get more productivity out of your team. We talked about the person who needs coaching and training and the person who may be in the wrong role but isn't completely failing. They both have strengths you can work with, but it's not enough to get your team to a 15 percent increase in productivity. You said your team didn't come up with any practical ideas. What about you? Do you have any solutions?"

"I've given this a lot of thought," Jennifer responds, "and bounced several ideas off my team. Because they're closer to the action, I wanted to know what they thought. I think I've found a couple of ways to make a difference. I'll share them with you."

Bill quickly clarifies, "I don't work in your area, so I'm probably not the best person to give you advice on how to make your team more productive. Here's what I propose. When's your first strategic planning meeting?"

"In a month," Jennifer says.

"Here's what you can do between now and then. To kick off your first strategic meeting, I suggest you roll out your plan to make the team more productive. You mentioned you have something in mind that you think could work. Use the next four weeks to write up your plan and create a pre-

It is important for mentors to know the limits of their expertise. Don't give advice on a topic or situation without being confident and experienced. Your guidance is priceless to the mentee.

sentation that will enable you to walk the team through it to get their buy-in. That will give you confidence, Jennifer, that you're on the right track. They'll act as your quality assurance department.

"I'll be available to help if you want to run anything by me. I'm happy to do that, but I think it makes more sense for you to work with people who know the issues better than me. Then you can present your plan to leadership.

"Jennifer, a lot of leaders, when faced with these types of situations, immediately think of reorganizing their team or letting go of certain people. I discourage you from reacting like that. In the end, it may turn out that way, but I believe it's the easy way out and, as a rule, not always effective. My guiding principle in these types of situations is to try to establish stability in the work environment. Any departmental changes that can cause stress to employees should be a last resort.

"Your department may not be organized ideally, and I can always help you evaluate the situation, but after going through the exercise I gave you, you realized that five of your seven team members are meeting or exceeding expectations, and two are close. It sounds to me like you can get those two people over the line, so please don't gravitate too hastily toward reorganization or changing team members. It's a management shortcut that often turns into a long road and should only be used as a last resort.

"Before we get together again, Jennifer," Bill continues, "think about getting the most out of your team. It's a key element of good leadership.

"Getting the most out of a person will vary, depending on the company and their position. Here at Flagler we value employee morale, productivity, and employee retention. Those are our primary values, so you want to keep an eye on them. In another company, it could be different.

"Getting the most out of a team doesn't mean everyone will do the same thing today as they did yesterday. The more transparent you are when migrating people to new roles and responsibilities, the more success you'll have. Keep an open mind about how to achieve your goals. Things will change, and new ideas will emerge. Speak with your peers outside the company about how they've met their challenges.

"There will always be the temptation to blame the previous boss or reorganize the department. I encourage you to do neither. You're the leader, and when people see you taking responsibility, you'll be perceived as being strong. There's an old leadership joke called 'The Three Envelopes.' Let me share it with you.

"A new CEO is transitioning into his new role. The CEO who was stepping down met with him privately and presented him with three numbered envelopes. 'Open these if you run up against a problem you don't think you can solve,' he told him.

"In the beginning, things went well for the new CEO, but after six months, sales took a downturn and became his first major challenge. Frustrated with what to do, he remembered the envelopes. He went to his drawer and took out the first envelope. The message read, 'Blame your predecessor.'

"At the next board meeting, the new CEO placed all the blame for declining sales on the former CEO, and the board accepted it since they weren't fond of the previous regime.

"About a year later, the company was losing market share due to start-up competitors. Remembering the envelopes, the CEO immediately opened the second envelope. The message read, 'Reorganize,' which he did. The company quickly rebounded.

"After several solid quarters, employees went on strike, and the CEO was blamed, so he closed the door and opened the third envelope.

"The message said, 'Prepare three envelopes.'

"I know this is making light of tough leadership situations, but the story highlights that an easy way out doesn't always exist. Every situation is unique.

"There may be times when reorganizing is the right thing to do, but it will put you and the team under tremendous stress. Whenever you go through a process like that, you want to be sure it's the last resort and that you're doing it for all the right reasons. You need to be aware that letting go of employees impacts their personal lives. It's your job as a leader to help everyone be as successful as possible. You always want to be sure that before you let anyone go, you've done everything you possibly can to help the individual fit in to the team.

"Jennifer, let's recap what we've talked about related to building a productive team:

- Focus on the balance between micro- and macroleadership. Know when to go into detail and when to give space.

- As a leader, your role is to constantly evaluate the quality and productivity of individual team members, along with the overall quality of the team.
- Including your team in key decisions can minimize anxiety and provide greater insight into possible solutions."

Chapter 8

——— ✴ ———

Create Relationships: Leading in the Outside World

Jennifer and Bill have been meeting on a regular basis to maintain focus on team development and leadership. Jennifer personally feels she's been on track with her vision, but she's beginning to feel anxious and contacts Bill.

They meet in Jennifer's office. When Bill arrives, he can see that Jennifer is not herself. She doesn't smile and has an expression of concern on her face, so they jump right in.

Jennifer is worried about noise she's heard through the grapevine that people feel she's in over her head, that her team isn't doing well, and that she's in the wrong role.

People are questioning not only her performance, but also her team's. Her anxiety is healthy. Whenever anyone feels their brand is negatively impacted, it's appropriate to feel stress and anxiety. If not, a leader wouldn't be sufficiently concerned about leading the team.

First Bill asks, "What do you think, Jennifer? How do you think you're doing, and how well do you think your team is performing?"

Jennifer reflects on the past couple of months. The team has met established company metrics. Morale is strong. The team adopted the changes she put in place to improve productivity, and they're having a positive effect, according to the feedback she receives. She shares her positive perspective.

Bill asks a second question, "How much time do you spend with your peers who are leaders, the people who direct the teams your team members' support? Do you spend any time with your internal customers? I'm also aware that your team works on projects that impact the company's customers. Have you spent time with any of our external customers?"

"I never thought that was a part of my role here," Jennifer immediately concedes. "I spend most of my time leading my team. As you advised, I often attend meetings with them so that I can see how they're doing and to microlead to some extent. If anything comes up in a meeting that needs attention, I follow up and offer guidance. I also spend time with customers when my team is involved in projects that impact them. I attend those meetings as well. I make sure to go in order to demonstrate the importance of those relationships and to show my support."

"It sounds to me, Jennifer, that you may only be going through the motions. You're acting more like a senior project manager in those meetings than a leader."

"That's true, Bill. I use those situations as an opportunity to watch my team in action."

"Jennifer, do you remember when we first met, that one of the first things we talked about was your culture and your brand? I explained that it played a big role in how people see you. Let me ask another question. Why did our relationship begin? Why did you reach out to me to be a mentor?"

Jennifer looks bewildered because she knows Bill has the answer to his question. It's another one of those times when Bill asks a question that he already knows the answer to. But she has learned that he always has a reason for asking the questions he does, so she plays along with him to see where he's going with his line of inquiry.

She responds, "I wanted to do better. I felt like I was doing a good job, but my boss didn't see it that way. I wanted to improve so I reached out to you."

Then suddenly Jennifer becomes annoyed with herself. She realizes that she had answered her own question and knew what was coming, Bill would reinforce what she'd already expressed.

Bill jumps in and shares, "Of course, we focused on your brand and your culture. You acknowledged that these were areas you needed to improve, but you were paying more attention to your work than how people were seeing you. It sounds like this could be happening again. You said yourself that you spend most of your time with your team, which is great. It will strengthen them, but you're seeing things through your own eyes only.

"I want to challenge you to do the same thing for your team as you did for yourself, to focus on its culture and brand. I think it's time you start thinking about how others view your department. Clearly, if you're concerned about what people are saying, that you're in over your head and your team is not performing at their best, and you tell me your metrics are great, then you have an image problem. Feedback from your direct leaders has been positive, and you know things are going well. Let's dig in to the team's image and figure out what's going on."

Jennifer feels good because she realizes that she had arrived at the same conclusion herself and only needed Bill as a sounding board. This conversation is contributing to her self-confidence. Before she met Bill, she wouldn't have been able to reach this answer.

Leadership must stay aware of the image a team presents to customers and partners. Great leadership always ensures that the external world views a team in a manner that it deserves. You and your team's brand and culture are now partners.

Bill continues, "You're rattled because you know you and the team are doing a good job, but your image and brand have taken a hit. It's upsetting because you don't think it's warranted, so let's take a deeper look. This is healthy anxiety that will serve you in minimizing the concern. Think of it as a compass pointing you in a direction of leadership.

"The first thing that strikes me is that you're expressing a lot of confidence in your team and the quality of work they're doing without being arrogant about it. And that's important to acknowledge. However, when people say a leader's team isn't doing well, they could mean any number of things. Maybe a person who was held accountable by one of your team members is resentful. Perhaps your team called out a weakness in another team. The person or team in question may have lacked maturity and became defensive instead of embracing the challenge.

"We can't be sure that everything we hear is warranted, which isn't to say there isn't an element of truth in the situation. Your team may, in fact, need to improve how they communicate shortcomings to others. Because it's part of the project management's function to hold people accountable, it's appropriate that your team members identify weaknesses. How they deliver the message is what's critical. This could be an excellent opportunity for them to work on that skill. Remember, if this situation is going to benefit you and your team, the source of the problem can't lie in other people. You need to see this as an opportunity for self-reflection and self-improvement.

> Leaders must accept perceptions of their team. It's the only way they know when to create change, be it internally, within the team, or externally on how the team interacts with the outside world.

"A key item that I can't stress enough is that when you look for feedback, you always stay open-minded to whatever you hear. While being defensive can protect your team, it won't enable you as the leader to get to the root cause of the concerns.

"Another possibility is that the team missed the mark one time. You've heard the expression: if ninety-nine times you do things right and the hundredth time you make a mistake, it's the mistake people will remember, not the ninety-nine times you did things right. If that's the case now, it's important that you remain steadfast. You don't want to let one mistake jeopardize the over-all confidence of the team. Remember, confidence lies within the team and stems from both your confidence and the customer's confidence in them. It encompasses 360 degrees.

"Jennifer, you and I have spent a lot of time talking about what success looks like. In our last conversation, we discussed ways you can make your team stronger and organize it in the best possible way. You know what success looks like from your perspective from within the team. Now you need to consider how others see and evaluate it. Their barometer of success may be different.

"As your next action item, I want you to consider what success look like from the point of view of your internal customers and partners.

"Also, I want to take a minute to explore whose opinion matters. Let's examine that. Whose opinion do you think matters most, Jennifer?"

Jennifer reflects a bit. It's a tough question for her because the function of her team is to support other departments by providing project management services. Their mission is to assist other leaders, staff, external customers, and partners. They provide services to a wide range of people.

Bill comments that he can see the wheels turning in Jennifer's head. "This isn't a trick question. There's only one answer."

Jennifer finally says, "I think senior leadership's opinion is most important."

"Why do you think that?"

"Because at the end of the day, they're the ones that everyone in the company looks up to. We all respect them. Their opinions matter more than any others."

"I completely understand where you're coming from," Bill allows. "Being part of the senior leadership team myself, I'm flattered you think our opinions mean so much. But I'll be honest with you, I think everyone's opinion matters."

"Everyone?" Jennifer counters. "That doesn't seem like a fair answer. How can I please everyone?"

"That's the challenge! Consider this scenario: If your team works with a group of staff members and they think your team isn't providing the appropriate service, they'll go to their leadership and share their opinion. Now, leadership may like what your team is doing, but if staff is not satisfied, it will have a negative impact. You want to make sure that the folks whom your team services are happy. Their opinion matters."

Bill continues, "Of course, as you mentioned, you want to make sure senior leadership is happy, too. They're the ones who fund your projects. It's challenging to have to keep everyone satisfied, but it also makes for a lot of fun. It gives you an opportunity for finding creative ways to create satisfaction in all types of people.

"We've covered a lot of important material today. I suggest we take a break and in a few weeks meet in my office. In the meantime, I'd like you to think about areas in which your team could potentially provide a higher level of external service. When I say a higher level, I'm referring to managing expectations around quality. Take time to give it some thought. How's that sound?"

Jennifer agrees. There is a lot to digest.

After a general check-in about the past few weeks, Bill launches into a discussion of how people outside Jennifer's department are viewing her.

"I'd like to share with you some ideas I have about public versus private personas. To my way of thinking, the concept of persona includes both how people view you and how you present yourself to others, and it deserves careful consideration on your part in the same way micro- and macroleadership did. I want you to be deliberate in the way you present yourself publicly and privately. When I say private, I'm referring specifically to your team. Your private persona, or the way you present yourself to your team, may be one way, and your public persona, the way you present yourself outside of your department, another way."

> With their teams, leaders can elevate their transparency and present a private persona. With customers and partners, leaders should increase their reservedness while also expressing more openness to feedback.

Jennifer jumps in, "But why do I need two different personas?"

"Good question," Bill returns. "I'm not asking you to be two different people. As we've spoken about before, you should always be genuine, honest, and ethical. What I'm referring to has more to do with the way you carry yourself and come across to others.

"I'm bringing up the concept of public versus private personas because I believe it's important to present yourself in a positive way and to distinguish between the transparency you have with your team versus other departments. I recommend you let your team see more of the real Jennifer. You can be more open about goals with them as a way to build trust. With a foundation of trust in place, you'll be able to share any shortcomings you encounter more freely and provide coaching or other assistance.

"With customers and your peer group, you'll want to be more reserved when you deal with problems or shortcomings. I'm not suggesting you avoid them, but you'll want to be less direct than with your team. It will require greater sensitivity to the situation at hand and more delicacy when communicating issues that need attention. You'll want to find a balance between being forthright and restrained.

"The personas represent two approaches for you to use when holding someone accountable. With peers, you should come across as helpful but not subservient and be open to feedback. You also want to be receptive to feedback in your public persona and create an atmosphere that welcomes input.

"With your team, you're the leader, so you want to welcome feedback but guard against too much feedback, which could lead to a loss of control. In either case, never be defensive. No one likes to work with a defensive person because it immediately shuts down dialogue.

"Your mission is to obtain accurate and honest information about how people respond to your team. You're the department's representative, or agent. Your job is to learn why people are saying the things they do. You want to uncover if there's any jealousy. Does someone not like it that your team is holding them accountable? Are there any personality conflicts? Any number of things could be happening, so it's important that you've established trusting relationships to get at the heart of what's going on, not just what people are willing to share. It's the leader's responsibility to establish relationships with your team's internal customers. Even if you don't like the information you receive, at least it will be accurate."

Jennifer appreciates what she's hearing from Bill. She understands that there is another side to her job that she hadn't thought about. She's put all her energy into working within the team, and now she realizes that she's her team's interface with other departments. She's their poster child. It's her responsibility to discover why people may be feeling the way they do.

Being an optimist, Jennifer expects that she'll mostly hear good things about her team, but she's aware that may not always be the case. She knows it's all part of the journey.

The more she thinks about it, the more the idea of a public and private personas makes sense to Jennifer. She'll need to wear two hats, depending on whom she's engaged with. With the team, she can be direct; with external people, more nuanced.

"Bill, how do you recommend I do this? It all sounds great, but how do I put what you've shared into practice?"

"The first thing I recommend," Bill responds, "is to develop a talk tract, or script, that describes what your team does. Though most people will probably know your team provides project management, not everyone may fully understand what that entails. Some people may think that project management is an unnecessary expense or a superfluous layer of management. You'll need to create an elevator pitch to set the record straight."

"What's an elevator pitch? I've heard the expression, but am not sure I know what it means," Jennifer asks.

"Think of it like this: Here at Flagler, we have ten floors in our building, so the elevator pitch would be the facts that you can convey about your team in the amount of time it takes to travel from the first floor to the tenth, or roughly thirty to forty-five seconds. That's a short elevator pitch to use when you don't have much time to deliver your message.

"Now think of visiting a client whose offices are in a fifty-story building, you'd have more time to make your points. That's why I want you to create a short and longer version of your pitch. Your ultimate goal is to have such a great, short elevator pitch that someone wants to know more, and you move to the longer pitch. And by the way Jennifer, the reference to floor numbers is only a metaphor. You can use a pitch anywhere, but thinking of an elevator is a great way to visualize the concept of delivering pitches of various lengths.

The elevator pitch should be of various durations and cover a variety of topics, including who you and your team are and key initiatives. The purpose of each pitch is to grab the listener's attention and stimulate a desire to know more.

"If you happened to run into my boss, for example, who will know I'm mentoring you, you could tell her what you do in forty-five seconds. If she wants to know more, then you could go into the longer pitch and include a short success story, too. Every time you make your pitch, you're selling your team.

"Secondly, I want you to create a list of ten people from outside your team with whom you could realistically sit down and have a conversation. They could be customers, partners, or other internal leaders. Pick three with whom you're most comfortable and have lunch with them in the next month. Your mission in these lunch meetings is to enhance these personal relationships and practice your elevator pitches. Find out what matters to them outside of work, like we did when we first met. Toward the end of lunch, you could ask for a favor, explaining that you're developing an elevator pitch and would like to try it out on them. It will give them an opportunity to help, which is a good way to build a relationship with someone new."

> Leaders should never eat alone. The goal is to use every opportunity to network on behalf of their teams and themselves. Relationship building is a key role for a leader. Never miss out on opportunities.

ONE MONTH LATER

"How did your lunch meetings go?" Bill asks when he and Jennifer get together a month later.

"They were great and very helpful," Jennifer reports. "I bet next you're going to want me to have lunch with the other seven people on my list!"

"Not quite yet, Jennifer. I do want you to reach out to the other seven people and ask to spend time with them, but I want you to work out the best way for that to happen with each person. One way or the other, get on their calendars. It could be coffee, grabbing a drink after work, lunch, or a visit to their office. I want you to be completely open to how the get-together can happen. The goal is the same—to build personal relationships and practice your elevator pitch.

"The way I handle this kind of outreach is to make a to-do list. I try to meet with some people on a monthly basis, others, quarterly, and I routinely schedule the time in my calendar. I do the same with people I'm mentoring, my peer group, and people in other departments. I also meet with people outside of work and schedule them consistently in the same way. There are a lot more than ten people on my list, so I don't always manage to see everyone, but most importantly, I make it a practice to never eat alone when I'm in the office. That's always been my goal."

"That makes sense. Every time I see you in the cafeteria, you're always sitting with someone," Jennifer reports.

"To be clear, as I already told you, I never eat with people who work for me. I deliberately sit with other people, and

I don't eat at my desk unless I absolutely have to. I put effort into building relationships. Even if I have to discuss something work related, I make sure I spend quality time with people.

"Before our time is up, Jennifer, let's recap what we've talked about in our last few meetings:

- You have a public and private persona;
- Your private persona refers to the way you present yourself to your team; be conscious of the fact that you're their leader and, consequently, be more transparent with them;
- Your public persona reflects who you are with people who aren't part of your team; it requires receptivity to feedback, avoiding defensiveness, a desire to acquire information, and the intention to positively influence customers and partners; the goal is to build trustworthy relationships and develop allies; be confident, not arrogant;
- Never eat alone; always make a conscientious effort to build relationships; and
- Relationships matter!"

Conclusion

Bill and Jennifer's relationship evolved over the years. Bill started running his ideas past Jennifer, and she helped him think through new concepts he was working on. The relationship blossomed to the point where they both felt they were helping each other. A transformation in the mentor/mentee relationship that leads to balance between the two, like the one Bill and Jennifer now have, is exciting and rewarding, and it signals to Bill that it's time to move on.

A mentor can only give so much. There comes a time when the mentoring relationship begins to lose its value. Bill knows that for Jennifer to continue to grow, she'll need a new mentor, and, for his part, there are plenty more people who could use his help.

When they get together next, Bill knows it will be their last official meeting. He's apprehensive at first because he values their relationship and wants to be sure he handles things in the best way.

Sticking to Bill's principle of never eating alone, they decide to meet over lunch. Their plan is to speak about integrating a new employee who will be joining Jennifer's team. About halfway through lunch, Bill shares his awareness that it's time for Jennifer to move on.

"Jennifer, you're doing a great job. You're excelling in all areas. Many of the things we discuss now are simply reinforcing what you already know. You understand what it means to be a leader. I think the next exciting thing for you to do is to find a new mentor."

The expression on Jennifer's face is one of surprise and disappointment at the same time, which means a lot to Bill. He knows she values their relationship as much as he does. His goal is to transition into a model based more on friendship than mentorship.

Bill continues, "We can still meet for lunch or grab coffee. I'll always be here to help you whenever I can, but now it's time for the formality of our mentoring relationship to end and for you to work with another person who can help you. I've shared all the tools and techniques I have. There are other leaders at Flagler and elsewhere who will be able to help you improve.

"I suggest you do a couple of things. First, find another mentor. I can help you in the process, and I am more than happy to introduce you to other individuals who may be appropriate. You want to find a mentor who can take you to the next step of professional growth. Think about skills you want to develop, and we'll find the right person to help.

"Second and more exciting, Jennifer, I want to challenge you to become a mentor. You're providing excellent leadership, and I think becoming a mentor will allow you to grow even more. Our relationship began because you were seeking professional development. The next step is for you to find someone who wants the same thing, and you know how to go about it—just start talking to people. Find individuals who are looking for assistance and offer a helping hand.

"Being a mentor will allow you to continue to grow professionally. Remember, if a leader stagnates, so will the team.

"In preparation, let's review the eight disciplines of the Leadership Manifesto."

Bill hands Jennifer a copy of the Leadership Manifesto that he brought for her. Together they go through it:

1. Be yourself and build your personal brand and culture. Consider how you want the world to see you.
2. Speak up and gain confidence. Having confidence is fundamental to providing leadership.
3. Get involved and grow outside of the work place. External community and professional organizations can help you grow professionally and be a training ground for leadership.
4. Give and serve. The opportunity to influence others in every context shows people who you are.
5. Accept responsibility through managing the individuals who report directly to you. Get to know them.
6. Lead the way. Remember you are managing a team of individuals, not simply a group. Foster cooperation.
7. Build structure. How do you get the most out of your team? There's always a better way.
8. Create relationships. Build trustworthy connections in the outside world.

After thanking one another, they head back to their daily work lives with a great memory in place.

A WORD TO THE READER

Thank you for reading this book. I hope it has inspired you to seek a mentoring relationship in your life.

Both being a mentor and receiving the guidance of a mentor provide a unique opportunity for developing leadership skills and becoming a better human being. Personally, it is incredibly rewarding to help people become all they can be. The experience has enriched my personal and professional life. I've had the pleasure of witnessing the many colleagues I've mentored rise within their companies and become outstanding individuals inside and outside of work.

The beauty of being a mentor is that you can support and guide an individual's growth without having the responsibility and stress associated with managing performance or evaluating deliverables. The motivation behind mentoring is different and rooted more in friendship than leading a team.

When I'm managing my team, I want to get the most I can out of everyone. Of course, I care that they do well and grow professionally, but the fact is, I'm the person who is held accountable for the quality and productivity of their efforts. With mentoring, there are no ulterior motives other than helping another individual achieve the very best they can.

As Bill so frequently reminded Jennifer, we all need to build our personal brand. Our brand is unique and can be whatever we want it to be. We shouldn't lose sight of how others are viewing us and what we believe to be true about ourselves. Managing our brand is an ongoing project that reflects how we've developed as an individual and a professional.

Regardless of where we are in our careers, even if we're in senior management, we should be on the lookout for a good mentor. I believe it's never too late to benefit from the assistance of another person who can further our growth. A future mentor could even be a person whom we once mentored ourselves. Mentoring is a valuable tool for continued growth at every stage of life.

Most importantly, I want to encourage you to consider becoming a mentor. Good mentors are scarce, and, as I hope I have made clear in this book, the rewards are substantial for all involved—the person who is mentored, the mentor, and the companies they work for. Mentoring grows great leaders, and great leadership is the backbone of every outstanding organization.

For more information about mentorship, please visit the Leadership Manifesto website: www.leadershipmanifesto. com. You will find tips on improving your mentoring techniques, insights into the value of leadership in today's world of work, and resources for people who don't have access to a mentor.

Thank you again for giving your gift of time to this book and to others.

—BILL

Acknowledgments

The world is a better place thanks to people who want to develop and lead others. What makes it even better are people who share the gift of their time to mentor future leaders. Thank you to everyone who strives to grow and help others grow. It is the business version of *The Lion King* song "Circle of Life."

To all the individuals I have had the opportunity to lead, be led by, or watch their leadership from afar, I want to say thank you for being the inspiration and foundation for *The Leadership Manifesto*.

Without the experiences and support from my peers and team at Ultimate Software, this book would not exist. You have given me the opportunity to lead a great group of individuals—to be a leader of great leaders is a blessed place to be. Thank you to Chad, Dan, Dave, Gretchen, JC, Laura, Patrick, Scott, and Susan.

Having an idea and turning it into a book is as hard as it sounds. The experience is both internally challenging and rewarding. I especially want to thank the individuals that helped make this happen. Complete thanks to Joanie, Randy Walton, Patrick O'Neill, Barbara Boyd, Carol Raphael, and Dan Bernitt.

Scott Scherr, thank you for being a leader I trust, honor, and respect. I will always welcome the chance to represent you. "Au Au Au!"

About the Author

BILL HICKS has over twenty-five years of leadership experience, more than half of which has been at the executive level. Currently, he serves as chief relationship officer and senior vice president of customer relationships at Ultimate Software, a leading human capital management provider. Bill has been recognized for his leadership excellence, most recently as the 2013 South Florida CIO of the year and in 2015 with the Florida Multicultural Leadership Award. A graduate of Florida State University, Bill has been mentoring team members throughout his career. To learn more about Bill and his advice to mentors and those who seek mentoring, visit: www.leadershipmanifesto.com.

CPSIA information can be obtained
at www.ICGtesting.com
Printed in the USA
LVOW10*0337171017

552706LV00002B/3/P